English Grammar for Students of Spanish

**The Study Guide
for Those Learning Spanish**

Third edition

**Emily Spinelli
University of Michigan-Dearborn**

The Olivia and Hill Press®

English Grammar for Students of French
English Grammar for Students of German
English Grammar for Students of Italian
English Grammar for Students of Russian
English Grammar for Students of Latin
English Grammar for Students of Japanese

Gramática española para estudiantes de inglés

ISBN 0-934034-22-2

CONTENTS

TO THE STUDENT

English Grammar for Students of Spanish explains the grammatical terms that are in your Spanish textbook and shows you how they relate to English grammar. Once you have understood the terms and concepts in your own language, it will be easier for you to understand your textbook. With simple explanations and numerous examples, this handbook compares English and Spanish grammar, pointing out similarities and differences.

Most teachers incoporate *English Grammar* into the class syllabus so you will know which pages to read before doing an assignment in your Spanish textbook. If you are selecting the pages yourself, check the detailed index for the terms and concepts you will need to understand for your assignment. When you finish a chapter in *English Grammar*, you can test your comprehension by doing the short Reviews and checking your answers against the Answer Key.

Tips for Studying a Foreign Language

It is generally accepted that the two most important elements in learning a foreign language are vocabulary and grammar. Words (vocabulary) and the way in which they are formed and combined (grammar) together make up the ideas or messages that people wish to communicate. As a student you must learn the vocabulary and grammar presented in the classroom and textbook. This will in turn allow you to develop the four skill areas of language: listening, speaking, reading, and writing.

The following suggestions will help you improve your ability to learn the vocabulary and grammar and to become a successful foreign language learner.

1. **PRACTICE IN SEQUENCE**—Your Spanish textbook presents material in a sequential fashion; that is, each chapter and section of each chapter present new material that depends upon previously learned material. You need to learn the material in the order that it is presented; make sure you understand each section before moving on to the next one. Remember that language learning is like building a house; each brick is only as secure as its foundation.

2. **DAILY PRACTICE**—Set aside a block of time each day for studying Spanish. Don't get behind. It's almost impossible to catch up because you need time to absorb the material and to develop the skills.

3. **Active practice**—Practice the textbook exercises out loud; silent reading will not develop your speaking skill. Follow your speaking practice with the written exercises of the workbook. In this way the writing reinforces your speaking and vice versa. It also helps you learn vocabulary and grammar forms.

4. **Listening practice**—Listen to the audio tapes in the school language laboratory or on your own tape player. Listen for short periods of time several times per week. Four fifteen minute sessions over four days are far more beneficial than one hour-long session.

5. **Memorization**—Memorization plays an important part in language learning. For instance, you will have to memorize vocabulary, verb conjugations, and grammar rules. Learning vocabulary and verb endings in the context of complete sentences is easier and more efficient than learning them in isolation. Before exams, use the vocabulary lists and verb charts of the textbook to check if you really know the material.

6. **Vocabulary**—In addition to the suggestions given under Memorization, here are some other means to learn vocabulary that students have found useful.

Write each word on a separate index card, Spanish on one side, English on the other.

Use index cards or pens of different colors. This can help you remember other useful information about the word: using blue for masculine nouns and red for feminine nouns will help you remember genders. (You can also use green for verbs, orange for adjectives, etc. to remember parts of speech.)

When learning the Spanish words, look at the English words. Say aloud the Spanish word that corresponds; then flip the card to check your answer. Shuffle the deck often so you see the English word cold (i.e., without remembering the word order).

7. **Proficiency**—The principle goal of your Spanish instruction is for you to be able to communicate with Spanish speakers and to function in a Spanish-speaking country. Learning vocabulary and grammar is not the end goal; it is a means to develop your proficiency in listening, speaking, reading, and writing. Keeping the goal in mind will help you see the purpose behind the exercises you do and will ultimately help make you a successful language learner.

Buena suerte,
Emily Spinelli

INTRODUCTION

When you learn a foreign language, in this case Spanish, you must look at each word in three ways.

1. The **meaning** of the word—Each English word must be connected to a Spanish word that has an equivalent meaning.

> The English word *book* has the same meaning as the Spanish word **libro.**

Words with equivalent meanings are learned by memorizing **vocabulary**. Sometimes two words are the same or very similar in both English and Spanish. These words are called **cognates** and are, of course, easy to learn.

Spanish	English
inteligente	intelligent
problema	problem
visitar	visit

Occasionally knowing one Spanish word will help you learn another.

> Knowing that **niño** means *boy* should help you learn that **niña** is *girl;* or knowing that **hermano** is *brother* should help you remember that **hermana** is *sister.*

Usually, however, there is little similarity between words and knowing one Spanish word will not help you learn another. As a general rule, you must memorize each vocabulary item separately.

> Knowing that *man* is **hombre** will not help you learn that *woman* is **mujer.**

In addition, there are times when words in combination take on a special meaning.

> The Spanish word **hacer** means *to make;* **cola** means *tail.* However, **hacer cola** means *to line up, to stand in line.*

An expression whose meaning as a whole (**hacer cola**) is different from the meaning of the individual words (**hacer** and **cola**) is called an **idiom.** You will need to pay special attention to idiomatic expressions in order to recognize them and use them correctly.

2. The **classification** of a word—English and Spanish words are classified in eight categories called **parts of speech.** Here is a list of the parts of speech used in Spanish.

noun	article
verb	adverb
pronoun	preposition
adjective	conjunction

Each part of speech has its own rules for spelling, pronunciation and use. You must learn to recognize what part of speech a word is in order to choose the correct Spanish equivalent and know what rules to apply. Look at the word *that* in the following sentences.

a. *That* girl is my sister.
b. There is the car *that* he bought.
c. We didn't talk about *that*.[1]

The English word is the same in all three sentences, but in Spanish three different words will be used because each *that* belongs to a different part of speech.

3. The **use** of a word—A word must also be identified according to the role it plays in the sentence. Each word, whether English or Spanish, plays a specific role. Determining this role or function will help you choose the correct Spanish equivalent and know which rules to apply. Here is a list of functions.

subject
direct object
indirect object
object of a preposition

Let us examine the function of the word *him* in the following sentences.

a. They don't see *him*.
b. I wrote *him* a letter.
c. Are you going with *him*?[2]

The English word is the same in all three sentences, but in Spanish three different words will be used because each *him* has a different function.

---

[1]a. Demonstrative adjective, see p. 116.
b. Relative pronoun, see p. 169.
c. Demonstrative pronoun, see p. 160.

[2]a. Direct object, see p. 132.
b. Indirect object, see p. 134.
c. Object of a preposition, see p. 136.

Careful

As a student of Spanish you must learn to recognize both the part of speech and the function of each word in a sentence. This is essential because words in a Spanish sentence have a great deal of influence on one another.

The new red ***shoes*** *are on the small round table.*

Los nuevos **zapatos** rojos están sobre la pequeña mesa redonda.

IN ENGLISH

The only word that affects another word in the sentence is *shoes,* which forces us to say *are.* If the word were *shoe,* we would have to say *is.*

IN SPANISH

The word for *shoes* (**zapatos**) not only affects the word for *are* (**están**), but also the spelling and pronunciation of the Spanish words for *the, new,* and *red.* The word for *table* (**mesa**) affects the spelling and pronunciation of the Spanish words *the, small,* and *round.* The only word not affected by another word is **sobre,** meaning *on.*

Since parts of speech and function are usually determined in the same way in English and in Spanish, this handbook will show you how to identify them in English. You will then learn to compare English and Spanish constructions. This will give you a better understanding of the explanations in your Spanish textbook.

1. WHAT IS A NOUN?

A **noun** is a word that can be the name of a person, animal, place, thing, event, or idea.

IN ENGLISH

Let us look at some different types of words that are nouns.

- a person professor, clown, student, girl, baby
  Dr. Smith, Bill, Mary

- an animal elephant, horse, snake, eagle
  Lassie, Bambi, Garfield, Teddy

- a place city, state, country, continent
  Madrid, Michigan, Mexico, South America

- a thing apple, lamp, dress, airplane
  the White House, a Cadillac

- an event graduation, shopping, marriage, skiing, birth
  or activity the Olympics, Thanksgiving

- an idea democracy, humor, hatred, elegance, time
  or concept love, justice, poverty

As you can see, a noun can be a word that names something tangible, that is, something you can touch, such as a *lamp, horse*, or *Cadillac*. A noun can also be a word that names something abstract or intangible that you cannot touch, such as *love, justice*, or *honor.*

A noun that does not state the name of specific person, place, or thing, etc. is called a **common noun**. A common noun does not begin with a capital letter, unless it is the first word of a sentence. All the nouns in the preceding list that are not capitalized are common nouns.

A noun that is the name of a specific person, place, thing, etc. is called a **proper noun**. A proper noun always begins with a capital letter. All the nouns in the preceding list that are capitalized are proper nouns.

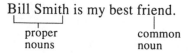

    Bill Smith is my best friend.
        proper   common
        nouns   noun

A noun that is made up of two or more words is called a **compound noun**. A compound noun can be a common noun such as *ice cream* or *comic strip*, or a proper noun, such as *South America* or *Mexico City.*

To help you learn to recognize nouns, look at the paragraph below where the nouns are in *italics*.

The *countries* that make up the Spanish-speaking *world* export *products* that we use every *day*. *Spain* produces many of the *shoes, purses,* and *gloves* that are sold in *stores* throughout the *United States*. *Spain* also sells us much *wine, sherry,* and *brandy*. The *islands* of the *Caribbean* and the *nations* of *Central America* supply us with tropical *fruits* such as *bananas* and *melons; sugar* is another important *export* of these *regions*. While *oil* is a major *source* of *income* for *Mexico* and *Venezuela,* the *economies* of several other *countries* of *Latin America* depend upon the *production* and *exportation* of *coffee*.

IN SPANISH
Nouns are identified in the same way they are in English.

Terms Used to Talk About Nouns

GENDER—A noun has gender, that is, it can be classified according to whether it is masculine, feminine, or neuter (see **What is Meant by Gender?**, p. 6).

NUMBER—A noun has number, that is, it can be identified according to whether it is singular or plural (see **What is Meant by Number?**, p. 10).

FUNCTION—A noun can have a variety of functions in a sentence; that is, it can be the subject of the sentence (see **What is a Subject?**, p. 26 or an object see **What are Objects?**, p. 132).

▼▼▼▼▼▼▼▼▼▼▼▼▼▼▼▼▼REVIEW▼▼▼▼▼▼▼▼▼▼▼▼▼▼▼▼▼

Circle the nouns in the following sentences.

1. The student came into the classroom and spoke to the teacher.

2. The Wilsons went on a tour of Mexico.

3. Figure skating is always an exciting event in the Winter Olympics.

4. Buenos Aires, the capital of Argentina, is a very cosmopolitan city.

5. Truth is stranger than fiction.

6. They want a manager with intelligence and a sense of humor.

?. WHAT IS MEANT BY GENDER?

... the grammatical sense means that a word can be classified as masculine, feminine, or neuter.

Gender is not very important in English. However, it is at the very heart of the Spanish language because the gender of a word often affects the way a word is spelled and pronounced. More parts of speech have gender in Spanish than in English as the list indicates.

English	Spanish
pronouns	nouns
possessive adjectives	pronouns
	articles
	adjectives

Since each part of speech follows its own rules to indicate gender, you will find gender discussed in the sections dealing with articles and the various types of pronouns and adjectives. In this section we shall only look at the gender of nouns.

IN ENGLISH
Nouns themselves do not have a gender, but sometimes their meaning will indicate a gender based on the biological sex of the person or animal named by the noun. When we replace a proper or common noun with *he* or *she,* we automatically use *he* for males and *she* for females. All the nouns that name things that do not have a sex are replaced by *it.*

Nouns referring to males indicate the **masculine** gender.

> Paul came home; *he* was tired, and I was glad to see *him.*
> noun   masculine   masculine
> male

Nouns referring to females indicate the **feminine** gender.

> The girl came home; *she* was tired and I was glad to see *her.*
> noun   feminine   feminine
> female

All other nouns which do not indicate a biological gender are considered **neuter**.

> The city of Washington is lovely. I enjoyed visiting *it.*
> noun   neuter

There are a few well-known exceptions, such as *ship,* which is referred to as *she.* It is custom, not logic, that decides.

The S/S United States sailed for Europe. *She* was a beautiful ship.

IN SPANISH

All nouns—common nouns and proper nouns—have a gender; they are either masculine or feminine. Do not confuse the grammatical terms "masculine" and "feminine" with the meaning of "male" and "female." Only a few Spanish words have a grammatical gender tied to whether they refer to someone of the male or female sex, most nouns have a gender that must be memorized.

The gender of nouns based on **biological gender** is easy to determine. These are nouns whose meaning is always tied to one or the other of the biological sexes, male or female.

Males → masculine	Females → feminine
Paul	Mary
boy	girl
brother	sister
stepfather	niece

The gender of all other nouns, common and proper, cannot be explained or figured out. These nouns have a **grammatical gender** that is unrelated to biological gender. Here are some examples of English nouns classified under the gender of their Spanish equivalent.

Masculine	Feminine
money	coin
book	library
country	nation
Peru	Argentina
dress	shirt
Wednesday	peace
sorrow	health
problem	philosophy

You will need to know the gender of every Spanish noun you learn. Gender is important not only for the noun itself, but for the spelling of the words it influences. Since a noun alone does not usually indicate its gender, when learning vocabulary, you will have to learn a noun with its article because the article does indicate gender (see **What are Articles?**, p. 12).

Endings Indicating Gender

Gender can sometimes be determined by looking at the end of the Spanish noun. In the lists that follow there are endings that often indicate feminine nouns and others that indicate masculine nouns. Since you will encounter many nouns with these endings in basic Spanish, it is certainly worthwhile to familiarize yourself with them.[1]

FEMININE ENDINGS

-a	la casa, la biblioteca	*house, library*
-dad, -tad	la ciudad, la libertad	*city, liberty*
-z	la nariz	*nose*
-ión, -ción	la reunión, la nación	*meeting, nation*
-umbre	la costumbre	*custom*
-ie	la especie	*species*

MASCULINE ENDINGS—Any ending except those provided in the "Feminine Endings" list. In particular:

-l	el papel	*paper*
-o	el libro	*book*
-n	el jardín	*garden*
-e	el parque	*park*
-r	el dolor	*pain*
-s	el interés	*interest*

To help you remember these endings note that for the masculine endings the letters spell "loners."

There are of course exceptions to the above rules: **la mano** (hand) and **el día** (day) are two common exceptions. Your textbook and instructor will point out the exceptions that you will need to learn.

---

[1]This table of endings has been adapted from John J. Bergen. "A Simplified Approach for Teaching the Gender of Spanish Nouns." *Hispania,* LXI (December, 1978), 875.

▼▼▼▼▼▼▼▼▼▼▼▼▼▼▼▼▼REVIEW▼▼▼▼▼▼▼▼▼▼▼▼▼▼▼▼▼

Circle M (masculine) or F (feminine) next to the nouns whose gender you can identify, and ? (unable to identIfy) next to the nouns whose gender you would have to look up in a dictionary.

1. boys   M   F   ?

2. chair   M   F   ?

3. Cathy   M   F   ?

4. classroom   M   F   ?

5. visitor   M   F   ?

6. sisters   M   F   ?

7. dresses   M   F   ?

3. WHAT IS MEANT BY NUMBER?

Number in the grammatical sense means that a word is singular or plural. When a word refers to one person or thing, it is said to be **singular**; when it refers to more than one, it is **plural**.

More parts of speech indicate number in Spanish than in English; there are also more spelling and pronunciation changes in Spanish as the following list indicates.

English	Spanish
nouns	nouns
verbs	verbs
pronouns	pronouns
only demonstrative	adjectives
adjectives	articles

Since each part of speech follows its own rules to indicate number, you will find number discussed in the sections dealing with articles, the various types of adjectives and pronouns, as well as in all the sections on verbs and their tenses. In this section we shall only look at number as it applies to nouns.

IN ENGLISH

A singular noun is made plural in one of two ways:

- a singular noun can add an *"-s"* or *"-es"*

book	book*s*
church	church*es*

- a singular noun can change its spelling

man	men
mouse	mice
leaf	leaves
child	children

A plural noun is generally spelled and pronounced differently from the singular.

Some nouns, called **collective nouns**, refer to a group of persons or things, but the noun itself is considered singular.

A football *team* has eleven players.
My *family* is well.
The *crowd* was under control.

IN SPANISH

As in English, the plural form of a noun is usually spelled differently from the singular.

- nouns that end in a vowel add "**-s**" to the singular noun

libro	libros	*book*	*books*
mesa	mesas	*table*	*tables*

- nouns that end in a consonant add "**-es**" to form a plural

papel	papel**es**	*paper*	*papers*
ciudad	ciudad**es**	*city*	*cities*

A few nouns will have internal spelling changes when they become plural. One such common change is "**-z**" to "**-c-**": **lápiz → lápices** (*pencil → pencils*). Your textbook will point out other exceptions to the two basic rules listed above.

Nouns do not change gender when they become plural.

▼▼▼▼▼▼▼▼▼▼▼▼▼▼▼▼▼▼REVIEW▼▼▼▼▼▼▼▼▼▼▼▼▼▼▼▼▼▼▼▼

Indicate if the following English and Spanish words are singular (S) or plural (P).

1. teeth   S   P

2. family   S   P

3. dress   S   P

4. mice   S   P

5. coches   S   P

6. mujer   S   P

4. WHAT ARE ARTICLES?

An **article** is a word placed before a noun to show whether the noun refers to a specific person, animal, place, thing, event, or idea, or whether the noun refers to an unspecified person, thing, or idea.

> I saw *the* boy you spoke about.
> a specific *boy*

> I saw *a* boy in the street.
> an unspecified *boy*

Definite Articles

IN ENGLISH

A **definite article** is used before a noun when we are speaking about a specific person, place, animal, thing, or idea. There is one definite article: *the*.

> I read *the* book you recommended.
> a specific *book*

> I ate *the* apple you gave me.
> a specific *apple*

The definite article remains *the* when the noun that follows becomes plural.

> I read *the* books you recommended.
> I ate *the* apples you gave me.

IN SPANISH

As in English, a definite article is used before a noun when referring to a specific person, place, animal, thing, or idea. However, in Spanish, the article works hand in hand with the noun it belongs to in that it matches the noun's gender and number. This "matching" is called **agreement**. (One says that the article *agrees* with the noun.) A different article is used, therefore, depending on whether the noun is masculine or feminine (gender) and depending on whether the noun is singular or plural (number). Because these articles are both pronounced and spelled differently, they indicate the gender and number of the noun to the ear as well as to the eye.

There are four forms of the definite article: two singular forms and two plural forms.

El indicates that the noun is masculine singular.

el libro	*the book*
el muchacho	*the boy*

La indicates that the noun is feminine singular.

la casa	*the house*
la muchacha	*the girl*

Los indicates that the noun is masculine plural.

los libros	*the books*
los muchachos	*the boys*

Las indicates that the noun is feminine plural.

las casas	*the houses*
las muchachas	*the girls*

The definite article is used much more frequently in Spanish than in English.

La química es difícil.
Chemistry is difficult.

Esa mujer es **la** señora Gómez.
That lady is Mrs. Gómez.

Memorize nouns with the singular definite article; in most cases the article will tell you if the noun is masculine or feminine.[1]

Indefinite Articles

An **indefinite article** is used before a noun when we are speaking about an unspecified person, animal, place, thing, event, or idea. There are two indefinite articles: *a* and *an*.

A is used before a word beginning with a consonant.[2]

I saw *a* boy in the street.
|
not a specific *boy*

---

[1]There are only a few exceptions to this statement. The primary exceptions are those feminine nouns that begin with a stressed **a-** and which for pronunciation purposes take **el** as the article: **el agua, el águila**. The noun is nonetheless still feminine: **el agua fría**.

[2]Vowels are the sounds associated with the letters *a, e, i, o, u* and sometimes *y*; consonants are the sounds associated with the other letters of the alphabet.

An is used before a word beginning with a vowel.

> I ate *an* apple.
> |
> not a specific *apple*

The indefinite article is used only with a singular noun; it is dropped when the noun becomes plural. At times the word *some* is used to replace it, but it is usually omitted.

> I saw boys in the street.
> I saw (*some*) boys in the street.
>
> I ate apples.
> I ate (*some*) apples.

IN SPANISH

As in English, an indefinite article is used in Spanish before a noun when referring to an unspecified person, animal, place, thing, event, or idea. Just as with definite articles, indefinite articles must agree with the noun's gender and number.

There are four forms of the indefinite article: two singular forms and two plural forms.

Un indicates that the noun is masculine singular.

> **un** libro   *a book*
> **un** muchacho   *a boy*

Una indicates that the noun is feminine singular.

> **una** casa   *a house*
> **una** muchacha   *a girl*

Unos indicates that the noun is masculine plural.

> **unos** libros   *some books*
> **unos** muchachos   *some boys*

Unas indicates that the noun is feminine plural.

> **unas** casas   *some houses*
> **unas** muchachas   *some girls*

Your textbook will instruct you on additional uses of the definite and indefinite articles in Spanish.

▼▼▼▼▼▼▼▼▼▼▼▼▼▼▼▼▼▼▼REVIEW▼▼▼▼▼▼▼▼▼▼▼▼▼▼▼▼▼▼▼

Below is a list of English nouns preceded by a definite or indefinite article. Write the Spanish article for each noun on the line provided. The Spanish dictionary entry shows you if that noun *(n.)* is masculine *(m.)* or feminine *(f.)*.

	Dictionary entry	**Spanish article**
1. the books	**libro** *(n. m.)*	_____
2. a table	**mesa** *(n. f.)*	_____
3. some classes	**clase** *(n. f.)*	_____
4. the telephone	**teléfono** *(n. m.)*	_____
5. a car	**coche** *(n. m.)*	_____
6. the sisters	**hermana** *(n. f.)*	_____
7. some men	**hombre** *(n. m.)*	_____
8. an apple	**manzana** *(n. f.)*	_____
9. the ball	**pelota** *(n. f.)*	_____

5. WHAT IS THE POSSESSIVE?

The term **possessive** means that one noun owns or possesses another noun.

> The book's pages are torn.
> | |
> possessor possessed
> singular plural

IN ENGLISH

You can show possession in one of two ways.

1. An apostrophe can be used. In this construction, the noun possessor comes before the noun possessed.

   ▪ a singular common or proper noun possessor adds an apostrophe + "s"

   > *Mary's* dress
   > |
   > singular possessor
   >
   > the *professor's* book
   > a *tree's* branches

   ▪ a plural possessor ending with "s" adds an apostrophe after the "s"

   > the *students'* teacher
   > |
   > plural possessor
   >
   > the *girls'* club

   ▪ a plural possessor not ending with "s" adds an apostrophe + "s"

   > the *children's* playground
   > |
   > plural possessor
   >
   > the *men's* department

2. The word *of* can be used. In this structure, the noun possessed comes before the noun possessor.

   ▪ a singular or plural common noun possessor is preceded by *of the* or *of a*

   > the book *of the* professor
   > the branches *of a* tree
   > |
   > singular common noun possessor
   >
   > the teacher *of the* students
   > |
   > plural common noun possessor

■ a proper noun possessor is preceded by *of*

the dress *of* Mary
             |
      proper noun possessor

IN SPANISH

The apostrophe structure does not exist. There is only one way to express possession and that is by using the "of" construction.

When a noun possesses another noun the structure is as follows: the noun possessed + **de**.

Mary's dress   →   *the dress of Mary*
| | | |
possessor noun   noun   possessor
        possessed   possessed

                           el vestido **de** María

the professor's book →   *the book of the professor*
                                el libro **del** profesor
                                      |
                                     de + el

the lady's purse   →   *the purse of the lady*
                               la bolsa **de la** señora

a tree's branches   →   *the branches of a tree*
                               las ramas **de un** árbol

the girls' father   →   *the father of the girls*
                               el padre **de las** muchachas

the boys' team   →   *the team of the boys*
                               el equipo **de los** muchachos

▼▼▼▼▼▼▼▼▼▼▼▼▼▼▼▼REVIEW▼▼▼▼▼▼▼▼▼▼▼▼▼▼▼▼▼▼

Below are possessives using the apostrophe. Write the alternate English structure that is the word-for-word equivalent of the Spanish structure.

1. some children's parents   _____

2. the doctor's office   _____

3. a car's speed   _____

4. the girls' soccer coach   _____

5. Gloria Smith's mother   _____

6. WHAT IS A VERB?

A **verb** is a word that indicates the action of the sentence. The word "action" is used in the broadest sense, not necessarily physical action.

IN ENGLISH
Let us look at different types of words which are verbs.

- a physical activity   to run, to hit, to talk, to walk
                            to wrestle

- a mental activity   to hope, to believe, to imagine
                            to dream, to think

- a condition   to be, to have, to seem

Many verbs however do not fall neatly into one of the above categories. They are verbs nevertheless because they represent the "action" of the sentence.

> The book *costs* only $5.00.
> |
>   to cost

> The students *seem* tired.
> |
>   to seem

To help you learn to recognize verbs, look at the paragraph below where the verbs are in *italics*.

> The three students *entered* the restaurant, *selected* a table, *hung* up their coats and *sat* down. They *looked* at the menu and *asked* the waitress what she *recommended.* She *advised* the daily special, beef stew. It *was* not expensive. They *chose* a bottle of red wine and *ordered* a salad. The service *was* slow, but the food *tasted* very good. Good cooking, they *decided, takes* time. They *ate* pastry for dessert and *finished* the meal with coffee.

The verb is one of the most important words in a sentence; you cannot write a **complete sentence**, i.e., express a complete thought, without a verb. It is important that you learn to identify verbs because the function of many words in a sentence often depends on their relationship to the verb. For instance, the subject of a sentence is the word doing the action of the verb, and the object is the word receiving the action of the verb (see **What is a Subject?,** p. 26 and **What are Objects?,** p. 132).

IN SPANISH
Verbs are identified the same way that they are in English.

Terms Used to Talk About Verbs

INFINITIVE—The verb form which is the name of the verb is called an infinitive: *to eat, to sleep, to drink* (see **What is an Infinitive?**, p. 20).

CONJUGATION—A verb is conjugated or changes in form to agree with its subject: *I do, he does* (see **What is a Verb Conjugation?**, p. 39).

TENSE—A verb indicates tense, that is, the time (present, past, or future) of the action: *I am, I was, I will be* (see **What is Meant by Tense?**, p. 58).

VOICE—A verb shows voice, that is, the relation between the subject and the action of the verb (see **What is Meant by Active and Passive Voice?**, p. 97).

MOOD—A verb shows mood, that is the speakers' attitude toward what they are saying (see **What is Meant by Mood?**, p. 73).

PARTICIPLE—A verb may also be used to form a participle: *writing, written, singing, sung* (see **What is a Participle?**, p. 66).

TRANSITIVE OR INTRANSITIVE—A verb can be classified as transitive or intransitive depending on whether or not the verb can take a direct object (see **What are Objects?**, p. 132).

▼▼▼▼▼▼▼▼▼▼▼▼▼▼▼▼REVIEW▼▼▼▼▼▼▼▼▼▼▼▼▼▼▼▼

Circle the verbs in the following sentences.

1. The students purchase their lunch at school.

2. Paul and Mary were happy.

3. They enjoyed the movie, but they preferred the book.

4. Paul ate dinner, finished his novel, and then went to bed.

5. It was sad to see the little dog struggle to get out of the lake.

6. I attended a concert to celebrate the new year.

7. WHAT IS AN INFINITIVE?

An **infinitive** is the name of the verb.

IN ENGLISH

The infinitive is composed of two words: *to* + the dictionary form of the verb (*to speak, to dance*). By **dictionary form**, we mean the form of the verb that is listed as the entry in the dictionary (*speak, dance*). Although the infinitive is the most basic form of the verb, it can never be used in a sentence without another verb which is conjugated (see **What is a Verb Conjugation?**, p. 39).

> *To learn* is exciting.
> └──┬──┘ │
> infinitive main verb

> It' s (it is) important *to be* on time.
>   │   └─┬─┘
>   main verb   infinitive

> Paul and Mary want *to dance* together.
>   │   └──┬──┘
>   main verb infinitive

> It has started *to rain*.
>   │   │   └─┬─┘
> auxiliary main infinitive
>   └──verbs──┘

The dictionary form of the verb, i.e., the infinitive without the *to,* is used after such verbs as *must* and *let.*

> Paul *must do* his homework.
>   │
>   dictionary form

> The parents *let* the children ***watch*** the television.
>   │
>   dictionary form

IN SPANISH

The infinitive form is composed of only one word that ends with the letters **-ar, -er**, or **-ir.** These letters are called the **infinitive endings**. The word *to* in the English infinitive has no Spanish equivalent.

habl**ar**	*to speak*
com**er**	*to eat*
viv**ir**	*to live*

These endings also tell you which group each verb belongs to:

-ar	→	1st group or conjugation
-er	→	2nd group or conjugation
-ir	→	3rd group or conjugation

It is important for you to identify the group to which a verb belongs so that you will know what pattern to follow when conjugating that verb.

In a sentence the infinitive form is always used for a verb that follows any verb other than **ser** *(to be)*, **estar** *(to be)*, or **haber** *(to have)*.

John and Mary want to dance together.
Juan y María quieren **bailar** juntos.
infinitive

It started to rain.
Empezó a **llover.**
infinitive

I can leave tomorrow.
Puedo **salir** mañana.
infinitive

You should study more.
Usted debe **estudiar** más.
infinitive

Notice that in the last two examples there is no "to" in the English sentence to alert you that an infinitive must be used in Spanish.

Careful

When looking up the equivalent of a verb in an English-Spanish dictionary, be sure to look for the specific meaning of the English verb. In English, it is possible to change the meaning of a verb by placing short words (prepositions or adverbs) after them. For example, the verb *look* in Column A changes meaning depending on the word that follows.

Column A		Column B
to look *for*	→	to search for
		I *am looking for* a book.
to look *after*	→	to take care of
		I *am looking after* the children.
to look *out*	→	to beware of
		Look out for lions.

In Spanish, it is generally not possible to change the meaning of a verb by adding a preposition or adverb as in Column A above. An entirely different verb would be used for each of the various meanings above. When consulting a dictionary, all the examples above under Column A will be found under the dictionary entry *look* (**mirar**), but you will have to search under that entry for the expression *look for* (**buscar**) or *look after* (**cuidar**) to find the correct Spanish equivalent. Don't select the first entry under *look* and then add on the Spanish equivalent for *after*; the result will be meaningless in Spanish.

▼▼▼▼▼▼▼▼▼▼▼▼▼▼▼REVIEW▼▼▼▼▼▼▼▼▼▼▼▼▼▼▼

Circle the words that you would replace with an infinitive in Spanish.

1. Mary has nothing more to do today.

2. The students must study their lesson.

3. Jeff wants to learn Spanish.

4. Mary can't sing very well.

5. We hope to travel through Spain this summer.

8. WHAT ARE AUXILIARY VERBS?

A **verb** is called an **auxiliary verb** or **helping verb** when it helps another verb form one of its tenses (see **What is Meant by Tense?**, p. 58). When it is used alone, it functions as a main verb.

Mary *is* a girl.	*is*	main verb
Paul *has* a headache.	*has*	main verb
He ***has been*** *gone* two weeks.	***has***	auxiliary verb
	been	auxiliary verb
	gone	main verb

IN ENGLISH

There are many auxiliary verbs, for example, *to have, to be,* and *to do*, as well as a series of auxiliary words such as *will, would, may, must, can, could* which are used to change the meaning of the main verb.

- An auxiliary verb is used primarily to indicate the tense of the main verb (present, past, future).

  Mary *is* reading a book.   **present**
  auxiliary *to be*

  Mary *has* read a book.   **past**
  auxiliary *to have*

  Mary *will* read a book.   **future**
  auxiliary *will*

- The auxiliary verb *to do* is used to help formulate questions and to make sentences negative (see **What are Declarative and Interrogative Sentences?**, p. 50 and **What are Affirmative and Negative Sentences?**, p. 47).

Does Mary read Spanish?	**interrogative sentence**
Mary *does not* read Spanish.	**negative sentence**

IN SPANISH

There are three verbs that can be used as auxiliary verbs: **haber** (*to have*), **estar** (*to be*), and **ser** (*to be*). The other auxiliaries such as *do, does, did, will,* or *would* do not exist as separate words. In Spanish their meaning is conveyed either by a different structure or by the form of the main verb. You will find more on this topic under the different tenses.

A verb tense composed of an auxiliary verb plus a main verb is called a **compound tense,** as opposed to a **simple tense** which is a tense composed of only the main verb.

Julia **estudia.**
simple tense
present of **estudiar**

Julia studies.

Julia **ha estudiado.**
auxililary   main
verb   verb
compound tense
present perfect tense of **estudiar**

Julia has studied.

Let us look at some examples of the compound tenses you will encounter in your study of Spanish.

PERFECT TENSES—The auxiliary verb **haber** *(to have)* followed by the past participle of the main verb is used to form the many perfect tenses (see p. 67 in **What is a Participle?** and **What are the Perfect Tenses?,** p. 82).

- present perfect tense → present tense of **haber** + past participle of main verb

  El hombre **ha comido** demasiado.
  auxiliary   main verb
  haber   **comer**

  The man has eaten too much.

- past perfect tense → imperfect tense of **haber** + past particple of main verb

  Los estudiantes ya **habían llegado.**
  auxiliary   main verb
  haber   **llegar**

  The students had already arrived.

You will learn other perfect tenses as your study of Spanish progresses.

PROGRESSIVE TENSES—The auxiliary verb **estar** *(to be)* followed by the present participle of the main verb is used to form the progressive tenses (see p. 66 in **What is a Participle?** and **What are the Progressive Tenses?,** p. 70).

- present progressive tense → present tense of **estar** + present participle of main verb

   Estoy leyendo un libro ahora.
   auxiliary   main verb
   estar   leer

   I am reading a book now.

- imperfect progressive tense → imperfect tense of **estar** + present participle of main verb

   Estábamos escuchando la radio.
   auxiliary   main verb
   estar   escuchar

   We were listening to the radio.

You will learn other progressive tenses as you continue your Spanish studies.

PASSIVE VOICE—The auxiliary verb **ser** *(to be)* is used to form the true passive voice (see **What is Meant by Active and Passive Voice?**, p. 97).

   El puente **fue construido** por los romanos.
   auxiliary   main verb
   ser   construir

   The bridge was constructed by the Romans.

▼▼▼▼▼▼▼▼▼▼▼▼▼▼▼▼REVIEW▼▼▼▼▼▼▼▼▼▼▼▼▼▼▼▼

Cross out the English auxiliaries that are not used as auxiliaries in Spanish.

1. We will go to Peru this year.

2. What are you doing?

3. Did you write your parents this week?

4. Tom had already graduated from high school by age sixteen.

5. Do you want to go to the movies with us?

9. WHAT IS A SUBJECT?

In a sentence the person or thing that performs the action is called the **subject**. When you wish to find the subject of a sentence, always look for the verb first; then ask, *who?* or *what?* before the verb. The answer will be the subject.[1]

Teresa speaks Spanish.

QUESTION: *Who* speaks Spanish? ANSWER: Teresa.
Teresa is the subject.

[Note that the subject is singular. It refers to one person.]

Are the keys on the table?

QUESTION: *What* is on the table? ANSWER: the keys.
Keys is the subject.

[Note that the subject is plural. It refers to more than one thing.]

Train yourself to ask that question to find the subject. Never assume a word is the subject because it comes first in the sentence. Subjects can be located in several different places, as you can see in the following examples (the *subject* is in boldface and *verb* is italicized):

*Did **the game** start* on time?
After playing for two hours, ***Paul** became* exhausted.
Looking in the mirror *was* a little ***girl**.*

Some sentences have more than one main verb; you have to find the subject of each verb.

The ***boys** were doing* the cooking while ***Mary** was setting* the table.

Boys is the subject of *were doing*.
[Note that the subject and verb are plural.]

Mary is the subject of *was setting*.
[Note that the subject and verb are singular.]

In both English and Spanish it is important to find the subject of each verb to make sure that the subject and the verb agree; that is, you must choose the form of the verb that goes with the subject. (See **What is a Verb Conjugation?**, p. 39.)

---

[1]The subject performs the action in an active sentence, but is acted upon in a passive sentence (see **What is Meant by Active and Passive Voice?**, p. 97).

▼▼▼▼▼▼▼▼▼▼▼▼▼▼▼▼REVIEW▼▼▼▼▼▼▼▼▼▼▼▼▼▼▼▼▼

Next to Q, write the question you need to ask to find the subject of the sentences below.
- Next to A, write the answer to the question you just asked.
- Indicate if the subject is singular (S) or plural (P).

1. When the bell rang, all the children ran out.

Q: _____

A: _____ S   P

Q: _____

A: _____ S   P

2. One waiter took the order and another brought the food.

Q: _____

A: _____ S   P

Q: _____

A: _____ S   P

3. The first-year students voted for the class president.

Q: _____

A: _____ S   P

4. That assumes I am always right.

Q: _____

A: _____ S   P

Q: _____

A: _____ S   P

5. They say that Spanish is a beautiful language.

Q: _____

A: _____ S   P

Q: _____

A: _____ S   P

10. WHAT IS A PRONOUN?

A **pronoun** is a word used in place of one or more nouns. It may stand, therefore, for a person, animal, place, thing, event, or idea.

For instance, rather than repeating the proper noun "Paul" in the following sentences, it is better to use a pronoun in the second sentence.

> *Paul* likes to swim. *Paul* practices every day.
> *Paul* likes to swim. *He* practices every day.

Generally a pronoun can only be used to refer to someone (or something) that has already been mentioned. The word that the pronoun replaces or refers to is called the **antecedent** of the pronoun. In the example above, the pronoun *he* refers to the proper noun *Paul. Paul* is the antecedent of the pronoun *he.*

IN ENGLISH

There are different types of pronouns, each serving a different function and following different rules. Listed below are the more important types and the sections where they are discussed in detail.

PERSONAL PRONOUNS—These pronouns change in form in the different persons and according to the function they have in the sentence.

- **subject pronouns** (see p. 30)

> *I* go.
> *They* read.
> *She* sings.

- **direct object pronouns** (see p. 139)

> John loves *her.*
> Jane saw *him* at the theater.

- **indirect object pronouns** (see p. 139)

> John gave *us* the book.
> My mother wrote *me* a letter.

- **object of preposition pronouns** (p. 139)

> Robert is going to the movies with *us.*
> Don't step on it; walk around *it.*

REFLEXIVE PRONOUNS—These pronouns refer back to the subject of the sentence (see p. 94).

> I cut *myself.*
> We washed *ourselves.*

INTERROGATIVE PRONOUNS—These pronouns are used in questions (see p. 153).

>*Who* is that?
>*What* do you want?

DEMONSTRATIVE PRONOUNS—These pronouns are used to point out persons or things (see p. 160).

>*This* (one) is expensive. *That* (one) is cheap.

POSSESSIVE PRONOUNS—These pronouns are used to show possession (see p. 165).

>Whose book is that? *Mine. Yours* is on the table.

RELATIVE PRONOUNS—These pronouns are used to introduce relative subordinate clauses (see p. 169).

>The man *who* is my instructor is very nice.
>This is the sweater *that* I bought last week.

INDEFINITE PRONOUNS—These pronouns are used to refer to unidentified persons or things.

>*One* doesn't do that.
>*Something* is wrong.

IN SPANISH

Pronouns are identified in the same way as in English and generally correspond in usage to their English equivalents. They can be studied in your textbook. The most important difference is that in Spanish a pronoun agrees with the noun it replaces; that is, it must correspond in gender and usually in number with its antecedent.

▼▼▼▼▼▼▼▼▼▼▼▼▼▼▼REVIEW▼▼▼▼▼▼▼▼▼▼▼▼▼▼▼

Circle the pronouns.
- Draw an arrow from the pronoun to its antecedent, or antecedents if there is more than one.

1. Did Mary call Peter? Yes, she called him last night.

2. That coat and dress are elegant but they are expensive.

3. Mary baked the cookies herself.

4. Paul and I are very tired. We went out last night.

5. If the book is not on the bed, look under it.

11. WHAT IS A SUBJECT PRONOUN?

A **subject pronoun** is a pronoun used as a subject of a verb.

He worked while *she* read.

QUESTION: Who worked? ANSWER: He.
He is the subject of the verb *worked.*

QUESTION: Who read? ANSWER: She.
She is the subject of the verb *read.*

Subject pronouns are divided into the following categories: the person speaking (the **first person**), the person spoken to (the **second person**), and the person spoken about (the **third person**). These categories are further divided into singular and plural.

	ENGLISH	SPANISH
singular		
lst person	I	**yo**
the person speaking		
2nd person	you	**tú**
the person spoken to		
3rd person	he	**él**
the person or object spoken about	she	**ella**
	it	
	(you)	**usted**[1]
plural		
lst person	we	**nosotros**
the person speaking plus others		**nosotras**
John and *I* speak Spanish. ⌞we⌟		
2nd person	you	**vosotros**
the persons spoken to		**vosotras**
Anita and *you* speak Spanish. ⌞you⌟		
3rd person	they	**ellos**
the persons or objects spoken about		**ellas**
John and *Anita* speak Spanish. ⌞they⌟	(you)	**ustedes**[1]

[1]**Usted/Ustedes** are logically 2nd person pronouns since they refer to the person spoken to. However, most Spanish textbooks group **usted/ustedes** with 3rd person pronouns since they take 3rd person verb endings. We have followed that pattern for ease of identification.

The English subject pronouns do not always correspond exactly to the Spanish subject pronouns. Let us look at the pronouns that are different so you can learn to choose the correct form.

"IT"

IN ENGLISH

Whenever you refer to the one thing or idea, you use the pronoun *it*.

Where is the book? *It* is on the table.
John has an idea. *It* is very interesting.

IN SPANISH

The subject pronoun *it* is not generally expressed. The verb ending indicates a third person singular; "it" is simply understood especially when the verb refers to a thing or an idea.

¿Dónde está el libro? **Está** sobre la mesa.

It is understod as part of the verb **está** since it refers to a thing
*Where is the book? **It is** on the table.*

Juan tiene una idea. **Es** muy interesante.

It is understood as part of the verb **es** since it refers to an idea.
*John has an idea. **It is** very interesting.*

"WE" → NOSOTROS, NOSOTRAS

IN ENGLISH

The word *we* refers to the person speaking plus others.

John and *I* are going to the movies.
We are leaving at 7:00.

IN SPANISH

There are two forms: **nosotros** and **nosotras. Nosotros** is used when "we" includes all males or a mixed group of males and females. **Nosotras** is used when the "we" includes only females.

Juan y yo vamos al cine. **Nosotros** salimos a las 7.
    | | |
masc. masc. or fem.   masc. subject
  └─antecedents ─┘   pronoun
John and I are going to the movies. We are leaving at 7:00.

María y yo vamos al cine. **Nosotras** salimos a las 7.
   | | |
fem.   fem.   fem. subject
└─antecedents─┘   pronoun
Mary and I are going to the movies. We are leaving at 7:00.

"THEY" → ELLOS, ELLAS

IN ENGLISH

Whenever you refer to more than one person or object, you use the plural pronoun *they.*

> My brothers play tennis. *They* practice every day.
> My sisters play soccer. *They* practice every day.
> Where are the books? *They* are on the table.

IN SPANISH

There are two forms: **ellos** and **ellas. Ellos** is used when "they" refers to all males or a mixed group of males and females. **Ellas** is used when "they" refers to all females.

> Mis hermanos juegan al tenis. **Ellos** practican todos los días.
>   masc. pl.   masc. pl.
>   antecedent   subject pronoun
>
> *My brothers play tennis.* ***They*** *practice every day.*

> Mis hermanas juegan al fútbol. **Ellas** practican todos los días.
>   fem. pl.   fem. pl.
>   antecedent   subject pronoun
>
> *My sisters play soccer.* ***They*** *practice every day.*

The subject pronoun "they" is not generally expressed when "they" refers to something other than people. The verb ending indicates a third person plural; "they" is simply understood.

> ¿Dónde están los libros? **Están** sobre la mesa.
> *They* is understood as part of the verb **están** since *they* refers to things.
> *Where are the books?* ***They are*** *on the table.*

"YOU" → TÚ, USTED, VOSOTROS, VOSOTRAS, USTEDES

As you can see there are several words for "you" in Spanish. **Tú** and **vosotros/vosotras** are called **familiar you**. **Usted** and **ustedes** are called **formal you**. To help you learn how to choose the correct form of *you* in Spanish an entire section has been devoted to **What is Meant by Familiar and Formal "You"?,** see p. 34.

▼▼▼▼▼▼▼▼▼▼▼▼▼▼▼▼REVIEW▼▼▼▼▼▼▼▼▼▼▼▼▼▼▼▼

Write the Spanish subject pronoun that you would use to replace the words in italics. If no pronoun is needed, write "0" in the space.

**Spanish
subject pronoun**

1. *I* am very tired. _____

2. *It* is very hot outside _____

3. *Mary* and *I* are leaving tomorrow. _____

4. My keys? I think *they* are on the table. _____

5. "Where do your parents live?"
   "*They* live in New Jersey." _____

6. *Gloria and Anita* are my best friends. _____

12. What is Meant by Familiar and Formal "You"?

IN ENGLISH
There is no difference between "you" in the singular and "you" in the plural. If you were in a room with many people and asked aloud, "Are you coming with me?" the "you" could refer to one person or many; it could also refer to close friends or complete strangers, the President of the United States or a dog.

IN SPANISH
There is a difference between "you" in the singular and "you" in the plural; there is also a difference between the "you" used with close friends, the familiar *you,* and the "you" used with persons you do not know well, the formal *you.*

Familiar "you" → tú, vosotros or vosotras
The familiar forms of *you* are used with members of one's family, friends, children, and pets. In general, you use the familiar forms with persons you call by a first name.

1. to address one person, male or female (singular) → **tú**

> Juan, ¿cómo estás **tú**?
> masc. sing.   familiar you
> *John, how are you?*

> María, ¿cómo estás **tú**?
> fem.   familiar you
> *Mary, how are you?*

2. to address more than one person (plural)

  ▪ a group of all males or a group of males and females → **vosotros**

> Juan y Pablo, ¿cómo estáis **vosotros?**
> masculine plural   familiar you
> *John and Paul, how are you?*

> Juan y María, ¿cómo estáis **vosotros?**
> masculine plural   familiar you
> *John and Mary, how are you?*

- a group of all females → **vosotras**

María, y Ana, ¿cómo estáis **vosotras?**
feminine plural   familiar you
Mary and Ann, how are you?

The plural familiar forms **vosotros** and **vosotras** are used only in Spain. In Latin America **ustedes** is used as the plural of **tú.** See below.

FORMAL "YOU" → USTED AND USTEDES

The formal forms of *you* are used to address persons you do not know well or persons to whom you should show respect. In general, you use the formal forms with persons you address with a title. Ms. Smith, Mr. Jones, Dr. Anderson, Professor Gómez.

1. to address one person male or female (singular) → **usted**

Señor Gómez, ¿cómo está **usted**?
masculine singular   formal you
Mr. Gómez, how are you?

Señora Gómez, ¿cómo está **usted**?
feminine singular   formal you
Mrs. Gómez, how are you?

2. to address more than one person, a group of males, females or mixed (plural) → **ustedes**

Profesor Gómez y Doctor García, ¿cómo están **ustedes**?
formal you   plural
Professor Gómez and Doctor García, how are you?

In Latin America **ustedes** is the plural of both the familiar and formal forms: **vosotros/vosotras** are not used. In Latin America **ustedes** would be used in the following situations.

Profesor Gómez y Doctor García, ¿cómo están **ustedes**?
formal you   masculine plural
Professor Gómez and Doctor García, how are you?

Juan y María, ¿cómo están **ustedes**?
familiar you   mixed group plural
John and Mary, how are you?

Ana y María, ¿cómo están **ustedes?**

familiar you   feminine plural

*Ann and Mary, how are **you?***

Here is a chart you can use as a reference.

ENGLISH			SPANISH	
			SPAIN	LATIN AMERICA
FAMILIAR	singular	*you*	tú	tú
	plural	*you*	vosotros vosotras	ustedes
FORMAL	singular	*you*	usted	usted
	plural	*you*	ustedes	ustedes

If you are in doubt as to whether to use the familiar or formal forms, use the formal forms unless speaking to a child or animal. The formal forms of *you* show respect for the person you are talking to and use of familiar forms can be considered rude if you do not know a person well.

To Choose the Correct Form of "You"

In order to choose the correct form of *you* in Spanish, you should ask yourself the following questions:

1. Do you need the familiar or formal form?

2. If you need the formal form:

   - Are you speaking to one person?
     Then the form is singular → **usted**
   - Are you speaking to more than one person?
     Then the form is plural → **ustedes**

3. If you need the familiar form:

   - Are you speaking to one person?
     Then the form is singular → **tú**
   - Are you speaking to more than one person?
     Then the form is plural, but the plural form you will choose depends on the region you are in.
   - Are you in Latin America?
     Then the form is the same as the formal plural form → **ustedes**
   - Are you in Spain?
     Then the form will depend on the gender of the group you are addressing.

- Are you speaking to a group of all males or males and females? Then the form is masculine → **vosotros**
- Are you speaking to a group of all females?
  Then the form is feminine → **vosotras**

Let's find the Spanish equivalent for you in the following sentences.

Mr. President, are you coming with us?

FAMILIAR OR FORMAL: Formal
SINGULAR OR PLURAL: Singular
Then the form is **usted**.

Señor Presidente, ¿viene **usted** con nosotros?

Mr. and Mrs. Lado, are you coming with us?

FAMILIAR OR FORMAL: Formal
SINGULAR OR PLURAL: Plural
Then the form is **ustedes**.

Señor y señora Lado, ¿vienen **ustedes** con nosotros?

John, are you coming with us?

FAMILIAR OR FORMAL: Familiar
SINGULAR OR PLURAL: Singular
Then the form is **tú**.

Juan, ¿vienes **tú** con nosotros?

Isabel and Gloria, are you coming with us?

FAMILIAR OR FORMAL: Familiar
SINGULAR OR PLURAL: Plural
SPAIN OR LATIN AMERICA: Spain
MALES OR MIXED GROUP OR ALL FEMALES: Females
Then the form is **vosotras**.

Isabel y Gloria ¿venís **vosotras** con nosotros?

Vincent and John, are you coming with us?

FAMILIAR OR FORMAL: Familiar
SINGULAR OR PLURAL: Plural
SPAIN OR LATIN AMERICA: Latin America
Then the form is **ustedes**.

Vicente y Juan ¿vienen **ustedes** con nosotros?

Below is a flow chart of the steps you have to follow to find the correct form of "you" in Spanish. It is important that you do the steps in sequence because each step depends on the previous one.

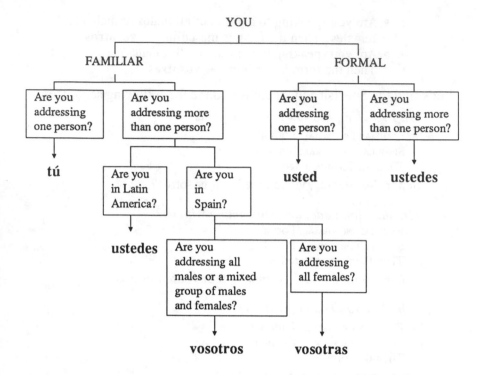

▼▼▼▼▼▼▼▼▼▼▼▼▼▼▼▼▼▼▼REVIEW▼▼▼▼▼▼▼▼▼▼▼▼▼▼▼▼▼▼▼

Write the form of "you" that would be used in each instance.

	Spain	Latin America
1. Mr. and Mrs. Fuentes, how are *you?*	_____	_____
2. Teresa, where are *you* going?	_____	_____
3. Señorita Acosta, will *you* please finish this report?	_____	_____
4. Come on children, *you* must go to bed.	_____	_____
5. Daddy, will *you* play a game with me?	_____	_____
6. Professor Suárez, *you* haven't given us our homework for tomorrow.	_____	_____

13. WHAT IS A VERB CONJUGATION?

A **verb conjugation** is a list of the six possible forms of the verb for a particular tense. For each tense, there is one verb form for each of the six persons used as the subject of the verb. (See **What is a Subject Pronoun?**, p. 30.)

IN ENGLISH

Most verbs change very little. Let us look at the various forms of the verb *to sing* when each of the possible pronouns is the subject.[1]

Singular

1st person   I *sing* with the music.

2nd person   You *sing* with the music.

               He *sings* with the music.

3rd person   { She *sings* with the music.

               It *sings* with the music.

Plural

1st person   We *sing* with the music.

2nd person   You *sing* with the music.

3rd person   They *sing* with the music.

Conjugating verbs in English is relatively easy because there is only one change in the verb forms; in the 3rd person singular the verb adds an "-s".

The English verb that changes the most is the verb *to be* which has three different verb forms in the present: *I am, you are, he/she is, we are, you are, they are.*

IN SPANISH

Verb forms change constantly, and it is therefore necessary to know the form of the verb for each of the six persons in each of the six persons in each tense. Memorizing all the forms of all the verbs that exist would be an impossible, endless task. Fortunately, most Spanish verbs belong to one of two categories.

Regular verbs are verbs whose forms follow a regular pattern. Only one example must be memorized and the pattern can then be applied to the other verbs of the same group.

Irregular verbs are verbs whose forms do not follow any regular pattern and must be memorized individually.

---

[1]In this section we will talk about the present tense only (see **What is the Present Tense?**, p. 60).

Subject

Pay special attention to the subject pronoun in this conjugation of the Spanish verb **cantar** *(to sing)*.

Singular

1st person	**yo**	canto
2nd person	**tú**	cantas
3rd person	**él** **ella** **usted**	canta

Plural

1st person	**nosotros** **nosotras**	cantamos
2nd person	**vosotros** **vosotras**	cantáis
3rd person	**ellos** **ellas** **ustedes**	cantan

Each subject represents the doer of the action of the verb.

1ST PERSON SINGULAR—The "*I* form" of the verb (the **yo** form) is used whenever the person speaking is the doer of the action.

>**Yo canto** mucho.
>*I sing a lot.*

Notice that **yo** is not capitalized except as the first word of a sentence.

2ND PERSON SINGULAR—the "*you* familiar form" of the verb (the **tú** form) is used whenever the person spoken to (with whom you are on familiar terms, p. 34) is the doer of the action.

>Juan, **tú cantas** muy bien.
>*John, you sing very well.*

3RD PERSON SINGULAR—the "*he, she, you* formal form" of the verb (the **él** form) is used when the person or thing spoken about is the doer of the action. The 3rd person singular subject can be expressed in one of four ways.

1. by the third person singular masculine pronoun **él** *(he)* and the third person singular feminine pronoun **ella** *(she)*

>**Él canta** muy bien.
>*He sings very well.*

Ella canta muy bien.
She sings very well.

2. by the singular pronoun **usted** *(you)*

Señor Gómez, **usted canta** muy bien.
Mr. Gómez, you sing very well.

Señorita Gómez, **usted canta** muy bien.
Miss Gómez, you sing very well.

The pronoun **usted** is generally abbreviated as **Ud.** The abbreviation is used far more frequently than the entire word.

3. by one proper name

María **canta** muy bien.
Mary sings very well.

Pedro **canta** muy bien.
Pedro sings very well.

El señor García **canta** muy bien.
Mr. García sings very well.

4. by a singular noun

El hombre **canta** muy bien.
The man sings very well.

La niña **canta** muy bien.
The girl sings very well.

El pájaro **canta** muy bien.
The bird sings very well.

The subject pronoun *it* has no Spanish equivalent. *It* as a subject is generally not expressed but rather understood as part of the verb. (See **What is a Subject Pronoun?**, p. 30.)

John has a new car. It's (it is) very nice.
Juan tiene un coche nuevo. **Es** muy lindo.

> *It* is understood as part of the verb *es.*

1ST PERSON PLURAL—The *"we form"* of the verb (the **nosotros** form) is used whenever "I" (the speaker) is one of the doers of the action; that is, whenever the speaker is included in a plural or multiple subject.

Nosotros **cantamos** bien.
We sing well.

Miguel, Gloria y yo **cantamos** muy bien.
nosotros
Miguel, Gloria and I sing very well.

> In this sentence *Isabel, Gloria and I* could be replaced by the pronoun *we*, so that in Spanish you must use the **nosotros** form of the verb.

2ND PERSON PLURAL—The "*you* familiar plural form" of the verb (the **vosotros** form) is used only in Spain when you are speaking to two or more persons with whom you would use **tú** individually.

Juan y tú **cantáis** muy bien.
Juan and you sing very well.

> In this sentence *John* (whom you would address with the **tú** form) and *you* could be replaced by the pronoun *you,* so that in Spanish you must use the **vosotros** form of the verb.

Many beginning Spanish textbooks do not emphasize or practice the **vosotros** form. Your instructor will inform you if you need to learn the **vosotros** forms of verbs or not.

3RD PERSON PLURAL—The "*they* or *you* formal form" of the verb (the **ellos** form) is used when the persons or things spoken about are the doers of the action. The 3rd person plural subject can be expressed in one of five ways:

1. by the third person plural masculine pronoun **ellos** *(they)* and the third person plural feminine pronoun **ellas** *(they)*

Ellos cantan muy bien.
They sing very well.

Ellas cantan muy bien.
They sing very well.

2. by the plural pronoun **ustedes** *(you)*

Elena y Francisco, **ustedes cantan** muy bien.
Elena and Francisco, you sing very well.

The pronoun **ustedes** is generally abbreviated as **Uds**. The abbreviation is used far more frequently than the entire word.

3. by two or more names

Isabel, Gloria y Roberto **cantan** muy bien.
ellos
Isabel, Gloria and Robert sing very well.

> In this sentence *Isabel, Gloria and Robert* could be replaced by *they* so that in Spanish you must use the **ellos** form of the verb.

La señora Gómez y la señora Jiménez **cantan** muy bien.

ellas

Mrs. Gómez and Mrs. Jiménez sing very well.

> In this sentence *Mrs. Gómez and Mrs. Jiménez* could be replaced by *they* so that in Spanish you must use the **ellos** form of the verb.

4. by two or more singular nouns

La chica y su padre **cantan** muy bien.

ellos

The girl and her father sing very well.

> In this sentence *the girl and her father* could be replaced by *they* so that in Spanish you must use the **ellos** form of the verb.

5. by a plural noun

> Las chicas **cantan** muy bien.
> *The girls sing very well.*

The subject pronoun *they* referring to things is generally not expressed but rather understood as part of the verb. (See **What is a Subject Pronoun?**, p. 30.)

> *Mary has new shoes. **They are** very nice.*
> María tiene zapatos nuevos. **Son** muy lindos.

> > *They* is understood as part of the verb **son** since *they* refers to a thing.

Verb Form

Let us again look at the conjugation of the same verb *to sing*, paying special attention to the verb forms. Notice that each of the six persons has a different verb form. However, when two or more pronouns belong to the same person, there is only one verb form. For instance, the 3rd person singular has three pronouns; **él**, **ella**, and **Ud.** but they all have the same verb form: **canta**.

yo	cant**o**
tú	cant**as**
él	
ella	} cant**a**
Ud.	

nosotros } cant**amos**
nosotras }

vosotros } cant**áis**
vosotros }

ellos }
ellas } cant**an**
Uds. }

The Spanish verb is composed of two parts.

1. The **stem** (also called the **root**) is formed by dropping the last two letters from the infinitive.

Infinitive	Stem
cant**ar**	cant-
com**er**	com-
viv**ir**	viv-

The stem will usually not change throughout a conjugation. However, in certain verbs called **stem-changing verbs**, the stem will change in a minor way.

2. The **ending** changes for each person in the conjugation of regular and irregular verbs. You will know which endings to add when you have established which group the verb belongs to.

Verb Groups

Regular verbs are divided into three groups, also called **conjugations**. The groups are identified according to the infinitive endings.

1st group	2nd group	3rd group
-ar	-er	-ir

Each of the three verb groups has its own set of endings for each tense (see **What is Meant by Tense?**, p. 58). You will need to learn the forms of only one sample verb from each group in order to conjugate any regular verb belonging to that group. As an example, let us look more closely at regular **-ar** verbs, that is, verbs like **hablar** *(to speak)* and **tomar** *(to take)* that follow the pattern of **cantar** *(to sing)* conjugated above.

1. Identify the verb group by its infinitive endings.

hablar   **-ar** verbs
tomar

2. Find the verb stem by removing the infinitive endings.

    habl-
    tom-

3. Add the ending that corresponds to the subject.

yo	hablo	yo	tomo
tú	hablas	tú	tomas

él		él	
ella	} habla	ella	} toma
Ud.		Ud.	

| nosotros | } hablamos | nosotros | } tomamos |
| nosotras | | nosotras | |

| vosotros | } habláis | vosotros | } tomáis |
| vosotras | | vosotras | |

ellos		ellos	
ellas	} hablan	ellas	} toman
Uds.		Uds.	

The endings for **-er** and **-ir** verbs will be different but the process of conjugation is always the same for regular verbs:

1. Identify the group of the verb by its infinitive ending.
2. Find the verb stem.
3. According to the group, add the ending that corresponds to the subject.

Omitting the Subject Pronoun

As you can see, in Spanish the verb ending indicates the subject. For instance, **hablo** can only have **yo** as a subject. Similarly, the subject of **hablas** can only be **tú**; the subject of **hablamos, nosotros**; the subject of **habláis, vosotros**.

Since you know the subject from the verb form, the subject pronoun is often omitted.

hablo	→	*I speak*
hablas	→	*you speak*
hablamos	→	*we speak*
habláis	→	*you speak*

If you do include the subject pronoun, it adds strong emphasis to the subject.

Yo canto.	→	*I sing (but he doesn't).*
Nosotros cantamos.	→	*We sing (but they don't).*

However, in the third person singular and plural it is often necessary to include the pronoun in order to avoid any doubt about who is the subject of the verb.

habla could be { **él** habla   *he speaks*
                    ella habla   *she speaks*
                    Ud. habla   *you speak*

hablan could be { **ellos** hablan   *they speak*
                      ellas hablan   *they speak*
                      Uds. hablan   *you speak*

The subject pronouns are included to clear up or clarify who is the subject in the above examples.

In many textbooks only the pronoun **nosotros** (instead of both **nosotros** and **nosotras**) will be listed in conjugations of new verbs. Likewise, only **vosotros** (instead of both **vosotros** and **vosotras**) will be listed.

▼▼▼▼▼▼▼▼▼▼▼▼▼▼▼▼REVIEW▼▼▼▼▼▼▼▼▼▼▼▼▼▼▼▼▼

Write the stem and conjugate the regular verb **comprar** *(to buy)*.

STEM: _____

yo	_____	nosotros	_____
tú	_____	vosotros	_____
él		ellos	
ella }	_____	ellas }	_____
Ud.		Uds.	

14. WHAT ARE AFFIRMATIVE AND NEGATIVE SENTENCES?

A sentence can be classified as to whether it states that a fact or situation is or is not true.

An **affirmative sentence** states that a fact or situation is true; it *affirms* the information it contains.

> Spain is a country in Europe.
> John will work in the university.
> They liked to travel.

A **negative sentence** states that a fact or a situation is not true; it denies or *negates* the information it contains. A negative sentence includes a word of negation such as *no, not,* or *nobody.*

> Spain is *not* a country in Asia.
> John will *not* work in a factory.
> They did *not* like to travel.

IN ENGLISH

An affirmative sentence can become a negative sentence in one of two ways:

1. by adding the word *not* after certain verbs

Affirmative	→	Negative
John is a student.		John is *not* a student.
Mary can do it.		Mary can*not* do it.
They will travel.		They will *not* travel.

Frequently, the word *not* is attached to the verb and the letter "o" is replaced by an apostrophe; this new word is called a **contraction.**

> John *isn't* a student.
> |
>   is not

> Mary *can't* do it.
> |
>   cannot

> They *won't* travel
> |
>   will not

Note that the contraction of *will not* is *won't.*

2. by adding the auxiliary verb *do, does*, or *did* + *not* + the dictionary form of the main verb. *Do* or *does* is used for negatives in the present tense and *did* for negatives in the past tense. (See **What is the Present Tense?**, p. 60 and **What is the Past Tense?**, p. 62.)

Affirmative	→	Negative
We study a lot.		We *do not study* a lot.
Julia writes well.		Julia *does not write* well.
The plane arrived.		The plane *did not* arrive.

Frequently *do, does*, or *did* form a contraction with *not*: *don't, doesn't*, or *didn't*.

IN SPANISH

The basic rule for turning an affirmative sentence into a negative sentence is much more simple than in English. You merely place **no** in front of the conjugated verb.

Affirmative	→	Negative
Estudiamos mucho.		**No** estudiamos mucho.
We study a lot.		*We **do not** study a lot.*
Julia escribe bien.		Julia **no** escribe bien.
Julia writes well.		*Julia **doesn't** write well.*
El avión llegó.		El avión **no** llegó.
The plane arrived.		*The plane **didn't** arrive.*

Careful

Remember that there is no equivalent for the auxiliary verbs *do, does*, or *did* in Spanish; do not try to include them in a negative sentence.

Negative Answers

When answering a question negatively in English, both *no* and *not* will often appear in the answer.

> *Do you live near the park?*
> *No, I do **not** live near the park.*

Since both *no* and *not* have the Spanish equivalent **no**, the word **no** will appear twice in the negative answer to that question in Spanish.

¿Vives cerca del parque?
No, no vivo cerca del parque.
   | |
no   not

> The first **no** answers the question; it has the English equivalent of *no*.
> The second **no** accompanies the verb; it has the English equivalent of *not*.

▼▼▼▼▼▼▼▼▼▼▼▼▼▼▼▼▼REVIEW▼▼▼▼▼▼▼▼▼▼▼▼▼▼▼▼▼

Write the negative of each sentence on the line provided.
- Circle the words that indicate the negative in the sentences you have just written.
- Place an "x" over the words that would not appear in the Spanish negative sentence.

1. We want to leave class early.

_____

2. He did his homework yesterday.

_____

3. Teresa will go to Chile this summer.

_____

4. Robert can go to the restaurant with us.

_____

5. Mr. Smith plays tennis every day.

_____

15. WHAT ARE DECLARATIVE AND INTERROGATIVE SENTENCES?

A sentence can be classified according to its purpose, whether it makes a statement or asks a question.

A **declarative sentence** is a sentence that is a statement; it *declares* the information.

> Columbus discovered America in 1492.

An **interrogative sentence** is a sentence that asks a question.

> When did Columbus discover America?

In written language, an interrogative sentence always ends with a question mark.

IN ENGLISH

A declarative sentence can be changed to an interrogative sentence in one of two ways:

1. by adding the auxiliary verb *do, does,* or *did* before the subject and changing the main verb to the dictionary form of the verb *(do* and *does* are used to introduce a question in the present tense and *did* to introduce a question in the past tense—see **What is the Present Tense?**, p. 60 and **What is the Past Tense?**, p. 62).

Declarative	→	**Interrogative**
Philip *likes* sports cars.		*Does* Philip *like* sports cars?
Paul and Mary *sing* together.		*Do* Paul and Mary *sing* together?
Mark *went* to Lima.		*Did* Mark *go* to Lima?

2. by inverting or switching the normal word order of subject + verb so the word order in the question is verb + subject

Declarative	→	**Interrogative**
Paul is home.		*Is Paul* home?

   Paul is home.
   subject — verb

   Is Paul home?
   verb — subject

   I am late.
   subject — verb

   Am I late?
   verb — subject

   She *will come* tomorrow.
   subject — verb

   Will she come tomorrow?
   subject — verb

IN SPANISH

A declarative sentence is changed to an interrogative sentence by placing the subject after the verb. The word order of the question is verb + subject.

Declarative	→	Interrogative
Juan estudia.		¿Estudia Juan?
John studies.		*Does John study?*
Los niños cantan.		¿Cantan los niños?
The children sing.		*Do the children sing?*

Notice that in written Spanish the question is signalled at both the beginning and end of the sentence. The punctuation mark at the beginning of the sentence looks like an upside-down question mark (¿); a question mark like the one in English is located at the end of the sentence (?).

Be sure to ignore the auxiliary verbs *do, does, did* when using Spanish. Spanish has no such helping verbs.

When a statement consists of a subject and verb plus one or two words, those few words are usually placed between the subject and the verb. The word order of the question is verb + remainder + subject.

Declarative → Interrogative

Juan estudia español.
subject verb
remainder

¿Estudia español Juan?
verb subject
remainder

John studies Spanish. *Does John study Spanish?*

La casa es grande.
subject verb
remainder

¿Es grande la casa?
verb subject
remainder

The house is big. *Is the house big?*

Los niños cantan bien.
subject verb
remainder

¿Cantan bien los niños?
verb subject
remainder

The children sing well. *Do the children sing well?*

Tag Questions

In both English and Spanish when you expect a yes-or-no answer to a question, you can transform a statement into a question by adding a short phrase to the end of the statement. This short phrase is often called a **tag** or a **tag question**.

IN ENGLISH

The tag question repeats the idea of the statement in a negative way.

> John is a nice guy, *isn't he?*
> We study a lot, *don't we?*

IN SPANISH

The words **¿no?**, **¿verdad?**, or **¿no es verdad?** can be added to the end of a statement to form a tag question.

> Juan es un buen chico, **¿no?**
> *John is a nice guy, **isn't he?***

> Trabajas mucho, **¿verdad?**
> *You work hard, **don't you?***

> Hoy es miércoles, **¿no es verdad?**
> *Today is Wednesday, **isn't it?***

▼▼▼▼▼▼▼▼▼▼▼▼▼▼▼▼REVIEW▼▼▼▼▼▼▼▼▼▼▼▼▼▼▼▼

Write the interrogative form of each declarative sentence on the line below.
- In the interrogative sentence, circle the English words that indicates the interrogative.
- In the interrogative sentence, put an "x" over the words that would not appear in the Spanish interrogative sentence.

1. Richard and Kathy studied all evening.

_____

2. Your brother eats a lot.

_____

3. The girl's parents speak Spanish.

_____

16. WHAT ARE SOME EQUIVALENTS OF "TO BE"?

IN ENGLISH

The verb *to be* has the following forms in the present tense: *I am; you are; he, she, it is; we are; you are; they are.* It is used in a variety of ways:

- for telling time

    It *is* 4:00.

- for discussing health

    John *isn*'t very well.

- for describing traits and characteristics

    Mary *is* tall and blond.

- for telling ages

    I *am* twenty years old.

- for explaining what there is or there are in specific places

    There *are* twenty-five students in the class.

IN SPANISH

There are various verbs used to express the English verb *to be*:

English	Spanish
to be	$\Big\{$ 1. **ser** *(to be)* 2. **estar** *(to be)* 3. **tener** *(to have)*
there is, there are	4. **hay** (a form of *to have*)

Depending on what you want to say, you will have to use one of these four verbs. Here are a few rules to help you select the correct one:

1. To be → "Ser"

You should use **ser** when you are speaking about the following:

- to tell time

    It is four o'clock.
    |
    time

    Son las cuatro.

- to show possession (see **What is the Possessive?**, p. 16)

> *That car is John's.*
> |
>   possession
> Ese coche **es** de Juan.

> *This book is yours.*
> |
>   possession
> Este libro **es** tuyo.

- to express nationality and origin

> *Mary is Spanish; she is from Madrid.*
> | |
>   nationality   origin
> María **es** española; **es** de Madrid.

- with nouns to identify someone or something

> *Mr. Robles is an engineer.*
> |
>   noun of identification
> El señor Robles **es** ingeniero.

> *That building is the language laboratory.*
>   └──────────┬──────────┘
>   noun of identification
> Ese edificio **es** el laboratorio de lenguas.

- with adjectives to describe traits or characteristics (see **What is an Adjective?**, p. 102)

> *Mary is tall and blond.*
>   └────┬────┘
>   adjectives describing traits
> María **es** alta y rubia.

2. To be → "Estar"

You should use **estar** when you are speaking about the following:

- to express location

> *John is in the library.*
>   └─────┬─────┘
>   location
> Juan **está** en la biblioteca.

*The books **are** on the table.*

　　　　　　　⌐————⌐
　　　　　　　location

Los libros **están** sobre la mesa.

- to discuss health

*How **are** you?*

⌐————————⌐
asking about health

¿Cómo **está** Ud.?

*Mary **is** fine but John **is** sick.*

　　　⌐————————⌐
　　　describing health

María **está** bien pero Juan **está** enfermo.

- with adjectives that describe a condition

*I **am** tired and worried.*

　　　⌐————————⌐
　　　adjectives of condition

Estoy cansada y preocupada.

"Ser" vs. "Estar"

The only situation in which both **ser** and **estar** can be used is when the verb *to be* is followed by an adjective. You will need to decide what type of adjective is used in order to correctly select a form of **ser** or **estar**.

- adjectives that describe traits and characteristics → **ser**

*My house **is** yellow.*

　　　　　　⌐
　　　　　　trait

Mi casa **es** amarilla.

> **Ser** is used because the adjective *yellow* distinguishes the house from others. It answers the question: Which house is yours?

*Mary **is** thin.*

　　　　　⌐
　　　　　trait

María **es** delgada.

> **Ser** is used because the adjective *thin* distinguishes Mary from other females. It answers the question: Which person is Mary?

▪ adjectives that describe conditions → **estar**

My house is dirty.
|
condition

Mi casa **está** sucia.

> **Estar** is used because the adjective *dirty* describes a special condition, not a normal characteristic of the house. It answers the question: What condition is the house in?

Mary is tired.
|
condition

María **está** cansada.

> **Estar** is used because the adjective *tired* describes a special condition not a normal characteristic of Mary. It answers the question: What is Mary's condition?

3. To be → "Tener" (to have)

The verb **tener** *(to have)* is sometimes used in expressions where English uses the verb *to be*. These expressions using **tener** must be memorized. Here are a few examples:

I am hungry.
|
to be

Tengo hambre.
|
to have ["I have hunger"]

I am twenty years old.
|
to be

Tengo veinte años.
|
to have ["I have twenty years"]

4. There is, there are → "Hay"

The English expressions *there is* or *there are* are translated with the Spanish word **hay**. **Hay** is used to explain the presence or absence of people or things in a particular place. **Hay** is invariable, that is, it does not change form since it can be either singular or plural.

There is a book on the table.
|
singular noun

Hay un libro sobre la mesa.

There are many books on the table.
|
plural noun

Hay muchos libros sobre la mesa.

You must learn to use this very common expression correctly and avoid using **estar** when you shouldn't. To avoid using the wrong form, see if you can replace the "is" or "are" of the English sentence with "there is" or "there are." If you can, you must use **hay;** if you can't, then **está** or **están** must be used to show location.

On the table *is* a book.
|
hay

You can say: On the table *there is a book.*

The book *is* on the table.
|
está

You can't say: The book *there is* on the table.

In the classroom *are* students.
|
hay

You can say: In the classroom *there are* students.

The chairs and tables *are* in the classroom.
|
están

You can't say: The chairs and tables *there are* in the classroom.

▼▼▼▼▼▼▼▼▼▼▼▼▼▼▼▼▼REVIEW▼▼▼▼▼▼▼▼▼▼▼▼▼▼▼▼▼

Decide if the *italicized* words are adjectives that describe a characteristic (CHAR) or a condition (COND). Then write the infinitive form of the verb you would use in Spanish.

	Adjective		Infinitive
1. My car is *gray.*	CHAR	COND	_____
2. My car is *dirty.*	CHAR	COND	_____
3. The students are *worried.*	CHAR	COND	_____
4. John is *tall, dark,* and *handsome.*	CHAR	COND	_____
5. I am *bored.*	CHAR	COND	_____
6. John, are you *sick?*	CHAR	COND	_____
7. Mary and I are *blond.*	CHAR	COND	_____

17. WHAT IS MEANT BY TENSE?

The **tense** of a verb indicates the time when the action of the verb takes place (at the present time, in the past, or in the future).

I am studying	**present**
I studied	**past**
I will study	**future**

As you can see in the above examples, just by putting the verb in a different tense and without giving any additional information (such as "I am studying *now,*" "I studied *yesterday,*" "I will study *tomorrow*"), you can indicate when the action of the verb takes place.

Tenses may be classified according to the way they are formed. A **simple tense** consists of only one verb form *(I studied)*, while a **compound tense** consists of two or more verb forms *(I am studying)*.

IN ENGLISH
Listed below are the main tenses whose equivalents you will encounter in Spanish.

Present
I study	**present**
I am studying	**present progressive**

Past
I studied	**simple past**
I have studied	**present perfect**
I was studying	**past progressive**
I had studied	**past perfect**

Future
I will study	**future**
I will have studied	**future perfect**

Conditional[1]
I would study	**conditional**
I would have studied	**conditional perfect**

As you can see, there are only two simple tenses (present and simple past). All of the other tenses are compound tenses formed by one or more auxiliary verbs plus the main verb (see **What are Auxiliary Verbs?**, p. 23).

---

[1]The conditional tenses have been included because they have parallels in English. The subjunctive tenses have been omitted because they have no parallels in English.

IN SPANISH

Listed below are the main tenses of the indicative mood that you will encounter in Spanish.

Present

estudio	*I study, I am studying* *I do study*	**present**
estoy estudiando	*I am studying*	**present progressive**

Past

estudié	*I studied*	**preterite**
estudiaba	*I used to study,* *I was studying*	**imperfect**
estaba estudiando	*I was studying*	**past progressive**
he estudiado	*I have studied*	**present perfect**
había estudiado	*I had studied*	**past perfect**

Future

estudiaré	*I will study*	**future**
habré estudiado	*I will have studied*	**future perfect**

Conditional

estudiaría	*I would study*	**conditional**
habría estudiado	*I would have studied*	**conditional perfect**

As you can see, there are more simple tenses than in English: present, preterite, imperfect, future, and conditional. The compound tenses in Spanish are formed with the auxiliary verbs **estar** (*to be*) or **haber** (*to have*) + the main verb.

This handbook discusses the various tenses and their usage in separate sections: **What is the Present Tense?**, p. 60; **What is the Past Tense?**, p. 62; **What is the Future Tense?**, p. 86; **What is the Conditional?**, p. 89; **What are the Progressive Tenses?**, p. 70; **What are the Perfect Tenses?**, p. 82.

18. WHAT IS THE PRESENT TENSE?

The **present tense** indicates that the action is happening at the present time. It can be:

- when the speaker is speaking
- a habitual action
- a general truth

I *see* you.

He *smokes* when he is nervous.

The sun *rises* every day.

IN ENGLISH

There are three forms of the verb that indicate the present tense although they have slightly different meanings.

Mary *studies* in the library.	**present**
Mary *is studying* in the library.	**present progressive**
Mary *does study* in the library.	**present emphatic**

When you answer the following questions, you will automatically choose one of the above forms.

Where does Mary study?
Mary *studies* in the library.

Where is Mary studying?
Mary *is studying* in the library.

Does Mary study in the library?
Yes, Mary *does study* in the library.

IN SPANISH

The simple present tense can be used to express the meaning of the English present, present progressive, and present emphatic tenses. In Spanish the idea of the present tense is indicated by the ending of the verb, without any auxiliary verb such as *is* and *does*. It is very important, therefore, not to translate these English auxiliary verbs. Simply put the main verb in the present tense.

*Mary **studies** in the library.*
present → **estudia**

*Mary **is studying** in the library.*
present progressive → **estudia**

*Mary **does study** in the library.*
present emphatic → **estudia**

▼▼▼▼▼▼▼▼▼▼▼▼▼▼▼▼▼REVIEW▼▼▼▼▼▼▼▼▼▼▼▼▼▼▼▼▼

Fill in the proper English form of the verb *to read* in the following sentences.
▪ Write the Spanish form for sentences 2 and 3.

1. What does Mary do all day?

   She _____   SPANISH VERB: **lee.**

2. Has she read *Don Quixote?*

   No, but she _____ it right now.   SPANISH VERB:_____

3. Does Mary read Spanish?

   Yes, she _____ Spanish.   SPANISH VERB: _____

19. WHAT IS THE PAST TENSE?

The **past tense** is used to express an action that occured in the past.

IN ENGLISH
There are several forms that indicate that the action took place in the past.

I worked	**simple past**
I was working	**past progressive**
I used to work	**with helping verb** used to
I did work	**past emphatic**
I have worked	**present perfect**
I had worked	**past perfect**

The simple past is called "simple" because it is a simple tense, i.e., it consists of one word (*worked* in the example above). The other past tenses are compound tenses; i.e., they consist of more than one word (*was working, did work,* etc.). The present and past perfect tenses are discussed in a separate section (see **What are the Perfect Tenses?**, p. 82).

IN SPANISH
There are several verb tenses that can be used to express an action that occurred in the past. Each tense has its own set of endings and its own rules that tell us when and how to use it. We are concerned here with only two of the past tenses in Spanish: the **preterite** ("el pretérito") and the **imperfect** ("el imperfecto").

The Preterite

The preterite is formed by adding certain endings to the stem. There are many irregular verbs in the preterite tense. It is very important to learn the preterite forms given in your textbook since the stems of the preterite are also used as the base for other verb forms.

The preterite generally translates as the simple past in English.

hablé → *I spoke*
estudié → *I studied*

The Imperfect

The imperfect is also formed by adding a set of endings to the stem. The conjugation is so regular (there are only three irregular verbs in the imperfect tense) that there is no need to repeat what is in your Spanish textbook. There are two English verb forms that indicate that the imperfect should be used in Spanish.

1. if the English verb form includes, or could include, the expression *used to*

> *When I was small, **I played** in the park.*
>
> > *I played* could be replaced by *I used to play*; therefore, the Spanish verb is put into the imperfect.
>
> Cuando yo era joven, **jugaba** en el parque.
> > imperfect

2. if the English form is in the past progressive tense, as in *was playing, were studying*

> *I **was studying** in my room.*
> Yo **estudiaba** en mi cuarto.

Except for these two verb forms, the English verb will not indicate to you whether you should use the imperfect or the preterite.

Selection of the Preterite or Imperfect

When discussing and describing past events and activities both the imperfect and preterite are used. You will have to learn to analyze sentences and their context so that you can decide which of the two tenses to use. As a general guideline, remember the following:

- **preterite** → tells "what happened" during a fixed time period
- **imperfect** → tells "how things used to be" or
  "what was going on" repeatedly over a period of time

As you will see in the two examples below, the tense of the verb in the answer will usually be the same as the tense of the verb in the question.

Let us consider the sentence "He went to Mexico." The same form of the verb, namely "went" is used in the two English answers below; however, the tense of the Spanish verb **ir** *(to go)* will be different depending on which question the verb answers.

- "What happened?"

  *What **did** Robert **do** last summer? He **went** to Mexico.*

    In this context you are asking and answering the question "what happened last summer"; therefore, the Spanish equivalent of the verbs "did do" and "went" will be in the preterite.

  ¿Qué **hizo** Roberto el verano pasado? **Fue** a México.
      preterite   preterite

- "How things used to be"

  *During his childhood, where **did** Robert **go** for the summer? He **went** to Mexico.*

    In this context, you are asking and answering the question "how things used to be"; therefore, the Spanish equivalent for the verbs "did go" and "went" will be in the imperfect.

  En su juventud, ¿adónde **iba** Roberto durante el verano?
                          imperfect

  Iba a México.
  imperfect

- "What was going on?"

  Since the imperfect and the preterite indicate actions that took place during the same time period in the past, you will often find the two tenses intermingled in a sentence or a story.

  *I **was reading** when **he arrived**.*

    Both actions "reading" and "arrived" took place at the same time.
    What was going on? I was reading   →   **imperfect**
    What happened?   He arrived   →   **preterite**

  Leía cuando **llegó.**
  imperfect   preterite

Your Spanish textbook will give you additional guidelines to help you choose the appropriate tense. You should practice analyzing English paragraphs. Pick out the verbs in a past tense and indicate for each one if, in Spanish, you would put it in the imperfect or preterite. Sometimes both tenses are possible, but usually one of the two will be more logical.

▼▼▼▼▼▼▼▼▼▼▼▼▼▼▼▼REVIEW▼▼▼▼▼▼▼▼▼▼▼▼▼▼▼▼

Circle the verbs that, in Spanish, would be put in the imperfect.
■ Underline the verbs that, in Spanish, would be put in the preterite.

Last summer, I went to Mexico with my family. Everyone was very
excited when we arrived at the airport. While my mother was
checking the luggage and my father was handling the tickets, my little
sister Mary ran away. My parents dropped everything and tried to
catch her, but she ducked behind the counter. Finally, a manager
grabbed her and brought her back to us. She was crying because she
was sad that she was leaving the dog for two weeks. Everyone comforted her and, finally, she smiled and got on the plane.

20. WHAT IS A PARTICIPLE?

A **participle** is a form of a verb which can be used in one of two ways: with an auxiliary verb to indicate certain tenses or as an adjective or modifier to describe something.

> I was *writing* a letter.
> auxiliary participle
> └─── past tense ───┘

> The *broken* vase was on the floor.
> participle describing *vase*

There are two types of participles: the **present participle** and the **past participle**. As you will learn, participles are not always used in the same way in English and Spanish.

The Present Participle

IN ENGLISH

The present participle is easy to recognize because it is an **-ing** form of the verb: *working, studying, dancing, playing*.

The present participle has two primary uses:

1. as the main verb in compound tenses with the auxiliary verb *to be* (see **What are the Progressive Tenses?,** p. 70)

> She is *singing*.
> present progressive of *to sing*

> They were *dancing*.
> past progressive of *to dance*

2. as an adjective

> This is an *amazing* discovery.
> describes the noun *discovery*

> He was a good *dancing* partner.
> describes the noun *partner*

IN SPANISH

The present participle is formed by adding **-ando** to the stem of **-ar** verbs and **-iendo** to the stem of **-er** and **-ir** verbs. The **-ndo** of the Spanish participle corresponds to the *-ing* of the English present participle.

Infinitive	Stem	Present participle
cantar	cant-	cant**ando**
comer	com-	com**iendo**
vivir	viv-	viv**iendo**

There are some irregular forms that you will have to memorize individually. The present participle is used primarily in the formation of the progressive tenses (see **What are the Progressive Tenses?**, p. 70).

Careful

Never assume that an English word ending in *-ing* will translate by its Spanish counterpart in **-ndo**. For example, after prepositions (see **What is a Preposition?**, p. 129) Spanish uses the infinitive form of the verb instead of a verb form ending in *-ing*.

After ***eating*** dinner, we went to the movies.
preposition
　　　　-ing form

Después de **cenar**, fuimos al cine.
preposition　infinitive

The Past Participle

IN ENGLISH

The past participle is formed in several ways. You can always find it by remembering the form of the verb that follows *I have:* I have *spoken*, I have *written*, I have *walked*.

The past participle has two primary uses:

1. as the main verb in compound tenses with the auxiliary verb *to have*

I *have written* all that I have to say.
He *hadn't spoken* to me since our quarrel.

2. as an adjective

> Is the *written* word more important than the *spoken* word?
>
> describes the noun *word*   describes the noun *word*

IN SPANISH

The past participle of regular verbs is formed using the following pattern: **-ar** verbs add **-ado** to the stem and **-er** and **-ir** verbs add **-ido** to the stem.

Infinitive	Stem	Past participle
hablar	habl-	hab**lado**
comer	com-	com**ido**
vivir	viv-	viv**ido**

You will have to memorize irregular past participles individually. As you can see from the following examples, the past participle may be very different from the infinitive.

Infinitive	Past participle
decir	dicho
escribir	escrito
poner	puesto
romper	roto

As in English the past participle can be used as part of a compound verb or as an adjective.

1. as the main verb in compound tenses with the auxiliary verb **haber** *(to have)* to indicate a perfect tense (see **What are the Perfect Tenses?**, p. 82)

> Los estudiantes han **terminado** la lección.
> *The students have finished the lesson.*

2. as an adjective

When the past participle is used as an adjective, it must agree with the noun it modifies in gender and number.

> the **closed** doors
>
> *Closed* modifies the noun *door*. Since **la puerta** *(door)* is feminine singular, the word for *closed* must be feminine singular. The participle must end **-a.**
>
> la puerta **cerrada**

*the **broken** records*

> *Broken* modifies the noun *records*. Since **los discos** *(records)* is masculine plural, the word for *broken* must be masculine plural. The participle must end in **-os**.

los discos **rotos**

▼▼▼▼▼▼▼▼▼▼▼▼▼▼▼▼▼REVIEW▼▼▼▼▼▼▼▼▼▼▼▼▼▼▼▼▼

Indicate the proper Spanish verb form for the words in italics: present participle (P), past participle (PP) or infinitive (I).

1. At 10:00 p.m. John was *watching* TV.   P   PP   I

2. We had already *gone* when Tom called.   P   PP   I

3. Barbara finished her homework before *going* out.   P   PP   I

4. An antique dealer near our house fixes
   broken dolls and toys.   P   PP   I

5. What are you *doing*?   P   PP   I

21. WHAT ARE THE PROGRESSIVE TENSES?

The **progressive tenses** are used to talk about actions that are in progress at a specific moment in time; they emphasize the moment that an action takes place.

> John *is talking* on the phone. [Right now.]
> We *were trying* to start the car. [At that moment.]

IN ENGLISH

The progressive tenses are made up of the auxiliary verb *to be* + the present participle of the main verb.

> We *are **leaving*** right now.
> | present participle of main verb *to leave*
> present tense of *to be*

> At that moment John *was **washing*** his car.
> | present participle of main verb *to wash*
>   past tense of *to be*

Notice that it is the tense of the auxiliary verb *to be* that indicates when the action of the main verb takes place.

IN SPANISH

The progressive tenses are made up of the auxiliary verb **estar** *(to be)* + the present participle of the main verb. A progressive form of the verb exists for all the tenses in Spanish. However, we shall here be concerned only with the present progressive. The present progressive is made up of the present tense of **estar** + the present participle of the main verb.

> **Estamos saliendo** ahora mismo.
> present tense   present participle
> of **estar**   of **salir** *(to leave)*
> *We are leaving right now.*

> **¿Estás comiendo** ahora?
> present tense   present participle
> of **estar**   of **comer** *(to eat)*
> *Are you eating now?*

Present vs. Progressive Tense

IN ENGLISH

The progressive tenses are used to describe habitual actions, to state general truths, and to describe an action that is happening at a specific moment. They are used far more frequently in English than in Spanish.

IN SPANISH

The progressive tenses are used only to emphasize an action that is happening at a particular moment or to stress the continuity of an action. The Spanish progressive tenses cannot be used to describe habitual action or to state general truths.

John, what **are** you **studying** in school?
present tense → **estudias**

The present tense is used in Spanish because you are asking what John is studying in general over a period of time.

John, what **are** you **studying** now?
present progressive → **estás estudiando**

The present progressive is used in Spanish because the word *now* indicates that you want to know what John is studying at this particular time as opposed to all other times.

Mary, **are** you **working** for the government?
present tense → **trabajas**

The present tense is used in Spanish because you are asking where Mary is working in general over a period of time.

Mary, **are** you **working** right now?
present progressive → **estás trabajando**

The present progressive is used in Spanish because the words *right now* indicate that you want to know if Mary is working at this particular time as opposed to all other times.

▼▼▼▼▼▼▼▼▼▼▼▼▼▼▼▼▼REVIEW▼▼▼▼▼▼▼▼▼▼▼▼▼▼▼▼▼▼

Indicate whether the Spanish version of the following English sentences would use the present tense (P) or the present progressive (PG).

1. This semester Robert *is studying* physics.   P   PG

2. Children, why *are* you *making* so much noise?   P   PG

3. I can't come to the phone. I *am getting* ready to go out.   P   PG

4. My brother *is working* for a computer firm in California. P   PG

5. My brother *is doing* very well.   P   PG

22. WHAT IS MEANT BY MOOD?

Verbs are divided into **moods** which, in turn, are subdivided into one or more tenses. The word "mood" is a variation of the word *mode* meaning manner or way. The various grammatical moods indicate the attitude of the speaker toward what he or she is saying. For instance, if you are making a statement you use one mood, but if you are giving an order you use another. As a beginning student of Spanish, you only have to recognize the names of the moods so that you will know what your Spanish textbook is referring to when it uses these terms. You will learn when to use the various moods as you learn verbs and their tenses.

IN ENGLISH

Verbs can be in one of three moods.

INDICATIVE—The indicative mood is used to state the action of the verb, that is, to *indicate* facts. This is the most common mood, and most of the verb forms that you use in everyday conversation belong to the indicative mood. Most of the tenses studied in this handbook belong to the indicative mood: the present tense (see p. 60), the past tense (see p. 62), and the future tense (see p. 86).

> Robert *studies* Spanish.
> present indicative

> Anita *was* here.
> past indicative

> They *will arrive* tomorrow.
> future indicative

IMPERATIVE—The imperative mood is used to give commands or orders (see **What is the Imperative?**, p. 78). This mood is not divided into tenses.

> Robert, *study* Spanish now!
> Anita, *be* home on time!

SUBJUNCTIVE—The subjunctive is used to express an attitude or feeling toward the action of the verb. Since it stresses feelings about the fact or the idea, it is "subjective" about them (see **What is the Subjunctive?**, p. 75). In English this mood is not divided into tenses.

> The school requires that students *study* Spanish.

I wish that Anita *were* here.
The teacher recommends that he *do* his homework.

IN SPANISH

The Spanish language identifies two moods: the indicative and the subjunctive.

INDICATIVE—As in English, the indicative mood is the most common, and most of the tenses you will learn belong to this mood.

SUBJUNCTIVE—The subjunctive mood is used much more frequently in Spanish than in English. The Spanish subjunctive has four tenses: present, imperfect, present perfect, and past perfect (also called the pluperfect). In addition, most imperative or command forms are also present subjunctive forms. Textbooks will use the term "present subjunctive" to distinguish that tense from the "present indicative."

23. WHAT IS THE SUBJUNCTIVE?

The **subjunctive** is a mood used to express a wish, hope, uncertainty, or other similar attitude toward a fact or an idea. Since it stresses the speaker's feelings about the fact or idea, it is usually "subjective" about them.

IN ENGLISH

The subjunctive is used in only a very few constructions. The subjunctive verb form is difficult to recognize because it is spelled like other forms of the verb.

> I *am* in Detroit right now.
> present indicative of *to be*
>
> I wish I *were* in Madrid right now.
> subjunctive spelled like past tense of *to be*

> He *reads* a book each week.
> present indicative of *to read*
>
> The professor insists that he *read* a book each week.
> subjunctive spelled like the dictionary form of *to read*

The subjunctive occurs most commonly in the subordinate clause of three kinds of sentences.

1. The subjunctive of the verb *to be (were)* is used in conditional clauses introduced by *if*.

> if clause   result clause
> If I *were* in Europe now, I would go to Madrid.
> subjunctive

> result clause   if clause
> John would run faster, if he *were* in shape.
> subjunctive

2. The same subjunctive form *were* is used in statements expressing a wish that is not possible.

> I wish I *were* in Europe right now.
> subjunctive

I wish she *were* my teacher.
|
subjunctive

3. The subjunctive of any verb, which is the same as the dictionary form of that verb, is used in the clause following expressions of necessity or demand, often with verbs of asking, urging, demanding, and requesting.

It is necessary that he *be* here.
|_____| |
    demand   subjunctive

I asked that she *come* to see me.
|_____| |
 request   subjunctive

IN SPANISH

The subjunctive is used very frequently, but unfortunately English usage will rarely help you decide where or how to use it in Spanish. Therefore, we refer you to your Spanish textbook. First, learn how to conjugate regular and irregular verbs in the present subjunctive. Then, learn the verbs and expressions that require you to put the verbs that follow into the subjunctive. Learn to form and use the other subjunctive tenses in the same way.

Following are some examples of a few of the types of expressions requiring the use of a subjunctive in Spanish.

- example of a verb of desire that is followed by a verb in the subjunctive: **querer** *(to want)*

    Quiero que Uds. **estudien** mucho.
    | |
    present indicative present subjunctive
    querer   **estudiar** *(to study)*

    *I want you **to study** a lot.*

    [word-for-word: *I want that you **study** a lot.*]

- example of an expression of doubt or uncertainty that is followed by a verb in the subjunctive: **dudar** *(to doubt)*

    Dudo que Roberto **llegue** hoy.
    | |
    present indicative present subjunctive
    dudar   **llegar** *(to arrive)*

    *I doubt that Robert **will arrive** today.*

    [word-for-word: *I doubt that Robert **arrives** today.*]

- example of an impersonal expression that is followed by a verb in the subjunctive: **es posible** *(it is possible)*

  Es posible que **compremos** un coche nuevo.

  > present subjunctive
  > **comprar** *(to buy)*

  *It's possible that **will buy** a new car.*

  [word-for-word: *It is possible that we **buy** a new car.*]

- example of a verb of advice or command that is followed by a verb in the subjunctive: **aconsejar** *(to advise)*

  Te aconsejo que **comas** muchas legumbres.

  > aconsejar   present subjunctive
  > **comer** *(to eat)*

  *I advise you **to eat** a lot of vegetables.*

  [word-for-word: *I advise that you eat a lot of vegetables.*]

- example of an expression of emotion that is followed by a verb in the subjunctive: **sentir** *(to be sorry)*

  Siento que Julio **esté** enfermo.

  > sentir   present subjunctive
  > **estar** *(to be)*

  I am sorry that Julio is sick.

▼▼▼▼▼▼▼▼▼▼▼▼▼▼▼▼▼REVIEW▼▼▼▼▼▼▼▼▼▼▼▼▼▼▼▼▼

Indicate the appropriate mood in Spanish for the verbs in italics: the indicative (I) mood or subjunctive (S) mood.

1. John wants Mary *to go out* with him.   I   S

2. I'm happy that you *got* a good job.   I   S

3. My mother says that Tom *is* a good student.   I   S

4. The doctor suggests that you *take* two aspirins
   for your fever.   I   S

5. It's important for you *to learn* Spanish.   I   S

6. We doubt that he *won* the lottery.   I   S

7. I know that John *lives* in that house.   I   S

24. WHAT IS THE IMPERATIVE?

The **imperative** is the command form of a verb. It is used to give someone an order. There are affirmative commands (an order to do something) and negative commands (an order not to do something).

IN ENGLISH

There are two types of commands, depending on who is being told to do, or not to do, something.

"YOU" COMMAND—When an order is given to one or more persons, the dictionary form of the verb is used.

Affirmative imperative	Negative imperative
Answer the phone.	*Don't answer* the phone.
Clean your room.	*Don't clean* your room.
Talk softly.	*Don't talk* softly.

Notice that the pronoun "you" is not stated. The absence of the pronoun *you* in the sentence is a good indication that you are dealing with an imperative and not a present tense.

You *answer* the phone.
 |
   present

Answer the phone.
 |
  imperative

"WE" COMMAND—When an order is given to oneself as well as to others, the phrase "let's" (a contraction of "let us") is used followed by the dictionary form of the verb.

Affirmative imperative	Negative imperative
Let's leave.	*Let's not leave.*
Let's go to the movies.	*Let's not go* to the movies.

IN SPANISH

As in English, there are also two basic types of commands, depending on whom is being told to do, or not to do, something. However, there are many forms of the *you* command to distinguish familiar and formal as well as affirmative and negative commands (see **What is Meant by Familiar and Formal "You"?**, p. 34).

"You" command

"Tú" command—When an order is given to someone to whom one says tú.

Affirmative imperative	Negative imperative
Habla.	No hables.
Speak.	*Don't speak.*
Ven aquí.	No vengas aquí.
Come here.	*Don't come here.*

The affirmative **tú** command has the same form as the third-person singular of the present indicative tense. There are also several irregular forms that you will have to learn individually. The negative **tú** command has the same form as the second-person singular of the present subjunctive.

"Vosotros" command—When an order is given to two or more persons with whom you say **tú** individually. The **vosotros** command is a familiar plural command and is used only in Spain.

Affirmative imperative	Negative imperative
Venid aquí.	No vengáis aquí.
Come here.	*Don't come here.*
Hablad.	No habléis.
Speak.	*Don't speak.*

The affirmative **vosotros** command is formed by dropping the **-r** from the infinitive ending and replacing it with the letter **-d**. The negative **vosotros** command has the same form as the second-person plural of the present subjunctive.

"Usted" command—When an order is given to a person with whom you say **usted**.

Affirmative imperative	Negative imperative
Hable.	No hable.
Speak.	*Don't speak.*
Venga aquí.	No venga aquí.
Come here.	*Don't come here.*

Both the affirmative and negative **usted** commands have the same form as the third-person singular of the present subjunctive.

"Ustedes" command—IN SPAIN: When an order is given to two or more persons with whom you use **usted** individually. IN LATIN AMERICA:

When an order is given to two or more persons with whom you use **tú** or **usted** individually.

Affirmative imperative	Negative imperative
Hablen.	**No hablen.**
Speak.	*Don't speak.*
Venga aquí.	**No venga** aquí.
Come here.	*Don't come here.*

Both the affirmative and negative **ustedes** commands have the same form as the third-person plural of the present subjunctive.

The use of **usted** or **ustedes** following the command is optional. It is considered somewhat more polite to use the pronoun, but it is not rude to omit it.

"We" command

The affirmative and negative **nosotros** command has the same form as the first-person plural of the present subjunctive.

Affirmative imperative	Negative imperative
Hablemos.	**No hablemos.**
Let's talk.	*Let's not talk.*
Salgamos.	**No salgamos.**
Let's leave.	*Let's not leave.*

Notice that the English phrase "let's" does not translate into Spanish; the command ending is the equivalent of "let's."

Here is a chart you can use as a reference for choosing the proper form of the Spanish command.

Command form	Affirmative	Negative
tú	present indicative 3rd pers. sing.	present subjunctive 2nd pers. sing.
vosotros	infinitive **-r → -d**	present subjunctive 2nd pers. pl.
usted	present subjunctive 3rd pers. sing.	present subjunctive 3rd pers. sing.
ustedes	present subjunctive 3rd pers. pl.	present subjunctive 3rd pers. pl.
nosotros	present subjunctive 1st pers. pl.	present subjunctive 1st pers. pl.

▼▼▼▼▼▼▼▼▼▼▼▼▼▼▼▼▼REVIEW▼▼▼▼▼▼▼▼▼▼▼▼▼▼▼▼▼

I. Change the following sentences to an affirmative command.

   1. You should study every evening.

   _____

   2. We go to the movies once a week.

   _____

II. Change the following sentences to a negative command.

   1. You shouldn't sleep in class.

   _____

   2. You aren't talking a lot.

   _____

III. Circle if the verb of the sentence is in the imperative (I) or the present (P).

   1. (estudiar) Estudien.   I   P

   2. (comer) No comas más.   I   P

   3. (escribir) Escriben cartas.   I   P

   4. (escuchar) Escuche al profesor. I   P

   5. (bailar) Bailemos.   I   P

   6. (leer) No lee mucho.   I   P

25. WHAT ARE THE PERFECT TENSES?

The **perfect tenses** are compound verbs made up of the auxiliary verb *to have* + the past participle of the main verb (see **What is a Participle?**, p. 66).

I *have* not *seen* him.
    │   │
   auxiliary past participle
   verb   of *to see*

They *had* already *gone.*
      │   │
    auxiliary past participle
    verb   of *to go*

The auxiliary verb *to have* can be put in different tenses. For example, *I have* is the present tense and *I have seen* is the present perfect tense. *They had* is the past tense and *they had gone* is the past perfect tense.

IN ENGLISH

There are four perfect tenses formed with the auxiliary verb *to have* + the past participle of the main verb. The name of each perfect tense is based on the tense used for the auxiliary verb *to have.*

PRESENT PERFECT—*to have* in the present tense + the past participle of the main verb (see **What is the Present Tense?**, p. 60).

I *have eaten.*
│   │
auxiliary past participle
verb   *to eat*

The boys *have washed* the car.
         │   │
      auxiliary past participle
      verb   *to wash*

PAST PERFECT (PLUPERFECT)—*to have* in the simple past + the past participle of the main verb (see **What is the Past Tense?**, p. 62).

I *had eaten* before 6:00.
│   │
auxiliary past participle
verb   *to eat*

The boys *had washed* the car before the storm.
        │   │
      auxiliary past participle
      verb   *to wash*

FUTURE PERFECT—*to have* in the future tense + the past participle of the main verb (see **What is the Future Tense?**, p. 86).

I *will have eaten* by 6:00.

    auxiliary   past participle
    verbs   *to eat*

The boys *will have washed* the car by Thursday.

        auxiliary   past participle
        verbs   *to wash*

CONDITIONAL PERFECT—*to have* in the conditional + the past participle of the main verb (see **What is the Conditional?**, p 89)

I *would have eaten* if I had had the time.

    auxiliary   past participle
    verbs   *to eat*

The boys *would have washed* the car if they had been here.

        auxiliary   past participle
        verbs   *to wash*

IN SPANISH

The perfect tenses are made up of a form of the auxiliary verb **haber** *(to have)* + the past participle of the main verb. In Spanish there are several perfect tenses: four perfect tenses in the indicative and two in the subjunctive (see **What is the Subjunctive?**, p. 75). As in English, the name of the tense is based on the tense of the auxiliary verb **haber.**

We are listing the various perfect tenses here so that you can see the pattern that they follow. You will see that an entire section is devoted to the perfect tenses, since they do not function in the same way in Spanish and English.

Perfect Tenses in the Indicative Mood

PRESENT PERFECT ("PERFECTO")—**haber** in the present tense + the past participle of the main verb. Generally the Spanish present perfect is used in the same way as the present perfect in English.

He comido.
I have eaten.

Los chicos **han lavado** el coche.
*The boys **have washed** the car.*

PLUPERFECT OR **PAST PERFECT** ("PLUSCUAMPERFECTO")—**haber** in the imperfect + the past participle of the main verb. The pluperfect tense is used to express an action completed in the past before some other past action or event. Generally, the Spanish past perfect is used the same way as the past perfect in English.

> **Había comido** antes de las seis.
> *I had eaten before 6:00.*

> Los chicos **habían lavado** el coche antes de la tempestad.
> *The boys had washed the car before the storm.*

FUTURE PERFECT ("FUTURO PERFECTO")—**haber** in the future + the past participle of the main verb. Generally, the Spanish future perfect is used in the same way as the future perfect in English.

> **Habré comido** para las seis.
> *I will have eaten by 6:00.*

> Los chicos **habrán lavado** el coche para el jueves.
> *The boys will have washed the car by Thursday.*

CONDITIONAL PERFECT ("CONDICIONAL PERFECTO")—**haber** in the conditional + the past participle of the main verb.

> **Habría comido** si hubiera tenido el tiempo.
> *I would have eaten if I had had the time.*

> Los chicos **habrían lavado** el coche si hubieran estado aquí.
> *The boys would have washed the car if they had been here.*

Perfect Tenses in the Subjunctive Mood
(See **What is the Subjunctive?**, p. 75)

PRESENT PERFECT SUBJUNCTIVE ("PERFECTO DEL SUBJUNTIVO")—**haber** in the present subjunctive + the past participle of the main verb. This tense is really just a present perfect used when a subjunctive is required.

> *He knows that they **have arrived**.*
>
> present perfect indicative → **han llegado**

> *He hopes that they **have arrived**.*
>
> present perfect subjunctive → **hayan llegado**

> A subjunctive is needed because *hopes* (the verb in the main clause) requires a subjunctive in the dependent clause.

PLUPERFECT SUBJUNCTIVE ("PLUSCUAMPERFECTO DEL SUBJUNTIVO")—**haber** in the imperfect subjunctive + the past participle of the main verb.

*He knew that they **had arrived**.*

pluperfect tense indicative → **habían llegado**

*He hoped that they **had arrived**.*

pluperfect subjunctive → **hubieran llegado**

A subjunctive is needed because *hoped* (the verb in the main clause) requires a subjunctive in the dependent clause.

▼▼▼▼▼▼▼▼▼▼▼▼▼▼▼▼REVIEW▼▼▼▼▼▼▼▼▼▼▼▼▼▼▼▼

Underline the verbs in a perfect tense.
- Indicate the tense of the verb underlined: present perfect (PP), past perfect (PSP), future perfect (FP) or conditional perfect (CP).

1. We had already gone when Teresa arrived.	PP	PSP	FP	CP
2. Barbara hasn't left yet.	PP	PSP	FP	CP
3. I will have graduated by next summer.	PP	PSP	FP	CP
4. We would have studied more if we had remembered the exam.	PP	PSP	FP	CP
5. Have you seen my new car?	PP	PSP	FP	CP

26. WHAT IS THE FUTURE TENSE?

The **future tense** indicates that an action will take place some time in the future.

IN ENGLISH

The future tense is formed with the auxiliary *will* or *shall* + the dictionary form of the main verb. Note that *shall* is used in very formal English (and British English); *will* occurs in everyday language.

> Paul and Mary *will do* their homework tomorrow.
> I *will leave* tonight.

In conversation *shall* and *will* are often shortened to *'ll:* They *'ll* do it tomorrow; I *'ll* leave tonight. *Will not* is often shortened to *won't:* They *won't* do it tomorrow; I *won't* leave tonight.

IN SPANISH

You do not need an auxiliary verb to show that an action will take place. Future time is indicated by a simple tense.

Regular verbs use the infinitive as a stem for the future tense.

Infinitive	Stem	
visitar	visitar-	*to visit*
comer	comer-	*to eat*
vivir	vivir-	*to live*

Irregular verbs have irregular future stems which must be memorized.

Infinitive	Stem	
venir	vendr-	*to come*
decir	dir-	*to say, tell*
saber	sabr-	*to know*

Your textbook will show you how to conjugate regular and irregular verbs in the future tense.

Substitutes for the Future Tense

In English and in Spanish the fact that an action will occur some time in the future can also be expressed without using the future tense itself but rather a structure that implies the future.

IN ENGLISH

You can use the verb *to go* in the present progressive + the dictionary form of the main verb: *I am going to travel, she is going to dance.*

similar meaning

I am going to travel.   I will travel.

present progressive   future tense
to go + infinitive

IN SPANISH

The same construction exists in Spanish. You can use the verb **ir** (*to go*) in the present tense + **a** + the infinitive.

similar meaning

Voy a viajar.   Viajaré.

present tense   future tense
ir + **a** + infinitive
I am going to travel. I will travel.

Note that the **a** has no English equivalent; it must appear in the Spanish sentence, however.

In conversational Spanish **ir a** + infinitive often replaces the future tense.

Sometimes the present tense is used to express a future idea especially when discussing a future event that is pre-arranged and certain to happen.

Mañana **tienen** un examen.

present tense

*Tomorrow you **will have** an exam.*

future tense

Future of Probability

In addition to expressing an action which will take place in the future, in Spanish the future tense can be used to express a probable fact, what the speaker feels is probably true. This is called the **future of probability.**

IN ENGLISH

The idea of probability is expressed with words such as *must, probably, wonder.*

My keys *must* be around here.
My keys are *probably* around here.
I *wonder* if my keys are around here.

IN SPANISH

It is not necessary to use the words *must, probably,* or *wonder* to express probable facts; the main verb is simply put into the future tense.

I wonder what time it ***is.***
　　present tense　　　　main verb → present tense

¿Qué hora **será?**
　　　main verb → future tense

It's probably 4 :00.
　main verb *is* → present tense

Serán las cuatro.
main verb → future tense

I can't find my book. Juan must ***have*** *it.*
　　　　　　　　main verb → present tense

No puedo encontrar mi libro. Juan lo **tendrá.**
　　　　　　　　　main verb → future tense

▼▼▼▼▼▼▼▼▼▼▼▼▼▼▼▼REVIEW▼▼▼▼▼▼▼▼▼▼▼▼▼▼▼▼▼

Circle the verbs in the following sentences.

- On the line provided, write the dictionary form of the English verb you would put in the future tense in Spanish.

Dictionary form

1. The students will study for the exam.　_____

2. I'll clean my room later.　_____

3. Shall we leave?　_____

4. I won't finish until tomorrow.　_____

5. Will she be here by 9:00?　_____

27. WHAT IS THE CONDITIONAL?

The conditional does not exist as a separate tense in English and some modern English grammar books do not include it. However, the conditional is a very important tense in Spanish. There is an English verb form which is similar to the Spanish conditional and which can help you understand it. For our purposes, we will call this form the "conditional." The conditional has a present and past tense called the **conditional** (present) and the **conditional perfect** (past).

Conditional

IN ENGLISH

The "conditional" is a compound tense. It is formed with the auxiliary *would* + the dictionary form of the main verb.

> I *would like* some ketchup, please.
> If she had the money, she *would call* him.
> I said that I *would come* tomorrow.

The conditional is used in the following ways:

- as a polite form with *like* and in polite requests

> I *would like* to eat.
>> This is more polite than "I want to eat."

> *Would* you please close the door.
>> The command "please close the door" is softened by *would*.

- in the main clause of a hypothetical statement

> If I had a lot of money, I *would buy* a Cadillac.

"I would buy a Cadillac" is a **clause** because it is composed of a group of words containing a subject *(I)* and a verb *(would buy)* and is used as part of sentence. It is called the **main clause** because it expresses a complete thought and can stand by itself without being attached to the first part of the sentence ("If I had a lot of money"). It is also called the **result clause** because it expresses what would happen as the result of getting a lot of money.

"If I had a lot of money" is called the **subordinate clause**, or **if-clause**. It is subordinate because, although as all clauses it contains a subject *(I)* and a verb *(had)*, it does not express a complete thought and cannot stand alone. It must be attached to the main clause.

The entire statement is called **hypothetical** because it refers to a condition that does not exist at the present time (the person speaking does not have a lot of money), but there is a remote possibility of its becoming a reality (the person speaking could have a lot of money some day).

- in an indirect statement to express a **future-in-the-past**

An **indirect statement** repeats, or reports, but does not quote, someone's words, as opposed to a direct statement which is a word-for-word quotation of what someone said. In written form a direct statement is always between quotation marks.

indirect statement	Paul said Mary would come.
	1 2
	past conditional
direct statement	Paul said, "Mary will come."
	1 2
	past future

In the indirect statement, action 2 is called a future-in-the-past because it takes placed after another action in the past, action 1. In the direct statement, action 2 is merely a quotation of what was said.

IN SPANISH

The conditional is a simple tense; you do not need an auxiliary verb to indicate it. The conditional is formed with the future stem (see p. 86) + the endings of the imperfect tense for **-er** and **-ir** verbs (**-ía, -ías, -ía, -íamos, -íais, -ían**).

Stem	Conditional	
hablar-	hablaría	*I would speak*
comer-	comería	*I would eat*
vivir-	viviría	*I would live*
pondr-	pondría	*I would put*
har-	haría	*I would do*

The conditional is used in the same ways as in English:

- as a polite form or in polite requests

> ¿**Podría** Ud. cerrar la puerta, por favor?
> conditional
> *Would you close the door, please?*

- in the main clause of a hypothetical statement to express what you would do under certain conditions

> Si tuviera mucho dinero, **compraría** una casa grande.
> conditional
>
> *If I had a lot of money, I would buy a big house.*

- in an indirect statement to express a future-in-the-past

> Dijo que **vendría.**
> conditional
> *He said that he would come.*

> Sabía que **llovería** esta noche.
> conditional
> *I knew that it would rain this evening.*

Conditional Perfect

IN ENGLISH
The **conditional perfect** is formed with the auxiliary *would have* + the past participle of the main verb.

> I *would have come* if I had known.

Unlike some statements in the conditional where there is a possibility of their becoming a reality, all statements using the conditional perfect are contrary-to-fact: the main action never happened because the condition expressed was never met and it is now over and done with.

> He *would have spoken* if he had known the truth.
> past conditional
>
> Contrary-to-fact: He did not speak because he did not know the truth.

> If you had called us, we *would have come*.
> past conditional
>
> Contrary-to-fact: We did not come because you didn't call us.

> I *would have eaten* if I had been hungry.
> past conditional
>
> Contrary-to-fact: I did not eat because I wasn't hungry.

IN SPANISH

The conditional perfect is formed with the auxiliary verb **haber** *(to have)* in the conditional tense + the past participle of the main verb: **habría salido** (see p. 67). As in English, statements using the conditional perfect are contrary-to-fact.

Si hubieran estudiado más, **habrían recibido** mejores notas.

conditional perfect

*If they had studied more, **they would have received** better grades.*

conditional perfect

Sequence of Tenses

Let us study some examples of constructions with conditions and their results so that you learn to recognize them and to use the appropriate Spanish tense.

Hypothetical and contrary-to-fact statements are easy to recognize because they are made up of two clauses:

- the **if-clause**; that is, the subordinate clause that starts with *if* (**si** in Spanish)
- the **result clause**; that is, the main clause

The sequence of tenses is sometimes the same in both Spanish and English. If you have difficulty recognizing tenses, just apply these three rules.

IF-CLAUSE → present tense   **RESULT CLAUSE** → future tense

*If **I have** time, **I will go** to the party.*

present   future

Si **tengo** tiempo, **iré** a la fiesta.

present   future

IF-CLAUSE → past tense **(English)**   **RESULT CLAUSE** → conditional
imperfect subjunctive **(Spanish)**

*If **I had** more time, **I would go** to the party.*

past   conditional

Si **tuviera** más tiempo, **iría** a la fiesta.

imperfect   conditional

subjunctive

IF-CLAUSE → past perfect (**English**)   RESULT CLAUSE → conditional perfect
  pluperfect subjunctive (**Spanish**)

> *If **I had had** more time, **I would have gone** to the party.*
>   └──┬──┘   └─────────┬─────────┘
>   past perfect   conditional perfect

> Si **hubiera tenido** más tiempo, **habría ido** a la fiesta.
>   └────────┬────────┘   └────┬────┘
>   pluperfect subjunctive   conditional perfect

In English and in Spanish the if-clause can come either at the beginning of the sentence before the main clause or at the end of the sentence. The tense of each clause remains the same no matter the order of the clauses.

> *I would have gone* to the party *if **I had had*** more time.
> └────────┬────────┘   └──┬──┘
> conditional perfect   past perfect

> **Habría ido** a la fiesta si **hubiera tenido** más tiempo.
> └────┬────┘   └────────┬────────┘
> conditional perfect   pluperfect subjunctive

▼▼▼▼▼▼▼▼▼▼▼▼▼▼▼▼▼REVIEW▼▼▼▼▼▼▼▼▼▼▼▼▼▼▼▼▼

For each of the verbs in italics, identify the tense you would use in Spanish: present (P), future (F), conditional (C), conditional perfect (CP), imperfect subjunctive (IS), or the pluperfect subjunctive (PS).

1. I know the children *would enjoy* that movie.

   P   F   C   CP   IS   PS

2. We *would go* to Spain if we *had* the money.

   P   F   C   CP   IS   PS

3. I *would like* some more meat, please.

   P   F   C   CP   IS   PS

4. If it *rains,* they *won't have* the picnic.

   P   F   C   CP   IS   PS

5. My parents wrote that they *would come* in July.

   P   F   C   CP   IS   PS

6. If I *had known* you were coming, I *wouldn't have left*.

   P   F   C   CP   IS   PS

28. WHAT IS A REFLEXIVE VERB?

A **reflexive verb** is a verb that is linked to a special pronoun called a **reflexive pronoun**; this pronoun serves to "reflect" the action of the verb back to the performer, that is, to the subject of the sentence. The result is that the subject and the object of the sentence are the same person.

>*She* cut *herself* with the knife.
>*He* saw *himself* in the mirror.

IN ENGLISH
Many verbs can take on a reflexive meaning by adding a reflexive pronoun.

>Peter *cuts* the paper.
> regular verb

>Peter *cuts himself* when he shaves.
> verb + reflexive pronoun

Pronouns ending with *-self* or *-selves* are used to make verbs reflexive. Here are the reflexive pronouns.

	Subject pronoun	Reflexive pronoun
singular	I	myself
	you	yourself
	he	himself
	she	herself
	it	itself
plural	we	ourselves
	you	yourselves
	they	themselves

In a sentence a reflexive pronoun is always tied to a specific subject, because both the pronoun and the subject refer to the same person or object.

>*I* cut *myself.*
>*Paul and Mary* blamed *themselves* for the accident.

Although the subject pronoun *you* is the same for the singular and plural, there is a difference between the reflexive pronouns used:

yourself is used when you are speaking to one person (singular) and *yourselves* is used when you are speaking to more than one (plural).

Paul, did you make *yourself* a sandwich?

Children, make sure you dry *yourselves* properly.

IN SPANISH

As in English, many regular verbs can be turned into reflexive verbs by adding a reflexive pronoun.

> Roberto **lava** el coche.
> *Robert washes the car.*

> Roberto **se lava**.
> *Robert washes himself.*

The dictionary lists **lavar** as the infinitive of *to wash* and **lavarse** as the infinitive of *to wash oneself*.

Here are the Spanish reflexive pronouns:

me	*myself*
te	*yourself* (fam. sing.)
se	*himself, herself, yourself* (form. sing.)
nos	*ourselves*
os	*yourselves* (fam. pl.)
se	*themselves, yourselves* (pl. fam. and form.)

Since the reflexive pronoun reflects the action of the verb back to the performer, the reflexive pronoun will change as the subject of the verb changes. You will have to memorize the conjugation of the reflexive verbs with the subject pronoun and the reflexive pronoun. For example, let's look at the conjugation of **lavarse** in the present tense. Notice that, unlike English, where the reflexive pronoun is placed after the verb, in Spanish the reflexive pronoun is placed immediately before the verb.

Subject pronoun	Reflexive pronoun	Verb
yo	me	lavo
tú	te	lavas
él ella Ud. }	se	lava

nosotros nosotras	}	nos	lavamos
vosotros vosotras	}	os	laváis
ellos ellas Uds.	}	se	lavan

Reflexive verbs can be conjugated in all tenses. The subject pronoun and the reflexive pronoun remain the same, regardless of the tense of the verb: **él se lavará** (future); **él se lavó** (preterite).

Careful

Reflexive verbs are more common in Spanish than in English; that is, there are many verbs that take a reflexive pronoun in Spanish but not in English. For example, when you say, "Mary washed in the morning," it is understood, but not stated, that "Mary washed *herself*." In Spanish the "herself" must be stated: "María **se lavó**." In addition, other English verbs such as *to get up* have a reflexive meaning. "Mary got up" means that she got herself up. In Spanish you express *to get up* by using the verb **levantarse**, that is **levantar** (*to raise*) + the reflexive pronoun **se** (*oneself*): "María **se levantó**." You must memorize the many verbs that require a reflexive pronoun in Spanish.

▼▼▼▼▼▼▼▼▼▼▼▼▼▼▼▼REVIEW▼▼▼▼▼▼▼▼▼▼▼▼▼▼▼▼

Fill in the proper reflexive pronoun in the Spanish sentences.

1. Mary always gets up early.

   María siempre _____ levanta temprano.

2. I worry about my family.

   Yo _____ preocupo por mi familia.

3. We have a good time at parties.

   Nosostros _____ divertimos en las fiestas.

4. You always complain about your classes.

   Tú _____ quejas siempre de tus clases.

29. WHAT IS MEANT BY ACTIVE AND PASSIVE VOICE?

The **voice** of the verb refers to a basic relationship between the verb and its subject. There are two voices: active and passive.

THE ACTIVE VOICE—A sentence is said to be in the active voice when the subject is the performer of the verb. In this instance, the verb is called an **active verb.**

> The teacher writes the exam.
> subject   verb   direct object

> Paul ate an apple.
> subject verb   direct object

> Lightning has struck the tree.
> subject   verb   direct object

In all these examples, the subject performs the action of the verb and the direct object is the receiver of the action.

THE PASSIVE VOICE—A sentence is said to be in the passive voice when the subject is the receiver of the action. In this instance, the verb is called a **passive verb.**

> The exam is written by the teacher.
> subject   verb   agent

> The apple was eaten by Paul.
> subject   verb   agent

> The tree was struck by lightning.
> subject   verb   agent

In all these examples, the subject is having the action of the verb performed upon it. The performer of the action, if it is mentioned, is introduced by the word *by.* The performer is called the **agent.**

IN ENGLISH

The passive voice is expressed by the verb *to be* conjugated in the appropriate tense + the past participle of the main verb. The tense of the passive sentence is indicated by the tense of the verb *to be.*

The exam *is written* by the teacher.

present

The exam *was written* by the teacher.

past

The exam *will be written* by the teacher.

future

IN SPANISH

As in English, a passive verb can be expressed by the auxiliary verb
ser (*to be*) conjugated in the appropriate tense + the past participle of
the main verb. The tense of the passive sentence is indicated by the
tense of the verb **ser.**

El examen **es** escrito por el profesor.

present

*The exam **is** written by the teacher.*

El examen **fue** escrito por el profesor.

preterite

*The exam **was** written by the teacher.*

El examen **será** escrito por el profesor.

future

*The exam **will be** written by the teacher.*

Note that all past participles agree in gender and number with the subject.

Esas **cartas** fueron **escritas** por el profesor.

fem. pl.   fem. pl.

*Those **letters** were **written** by the teacher.*

Careful

Be careful not to confuse a passive sentence in the past tense with an
active sentence in the present perfect. For instance, **ha cerrado** is the
present perfect of the verb **cerrar** (*to close*) and **fue cerrado** is the
past passive. As you can see in the following examples, the same
changes occur in English.

active   *The teacher **has written** the exam.*

⌐ auxiliary *to have* → present perfect

passive   *The exam **was written** by the teacher.*

⌐ auxiliary *to be* → past passive

active   El profesor **ha escrito** el examen.

⌐ auxiliary *to have* → present perfect

passive   El examen **fue escrito** por el profesor.

⌐ auxiliary *to be* → past passive

Changing an Active Sentence to a Passive Sentence

The steps to change an active sentence to a passive sentence are the same in English and in Spanish.

1. The direct object of the active sentence becomes the subject of the passive sentence.

active   The teacher writes the *exam.*

direct object

passive   *The exam* is written by the teacher.

subject

2. The tense of the verb of the active sentence is reflected in the tense of the verb *to be* in the passive sentence.

active   The teacher *writes* the exam.

present

passive   The exam *is* written by the teacher.

present

active   The teacher *wrote* the exam.

past

passive   The exam *was* written by the teacher.

past

active   The teacher *will* write the exam.

future

passive   The exam *will be* written by the teacher.

future

3. The subject of the active sentence becomes the agent of the passive sentence introduced with *by*. The agent is often omitted.

active   The *teacher* writes the exam.
            subject

passive   The exam is written by the *teacher.*
                                        agent

Avoiding the Passive Voice in Spanish

Although Spanish has a passive voice, it does not favor its use as English does, and whenever possible Spanish speakers try to avoid the passive construction by replacing it with an active one. This is particulary true for general statements, that is, when we don't know who is doing the action.

English is spoken in many countries.
    [We don't know who is speaking.]
The office opens at 9:00.
    [We don't know who is opening the office.]

There are two ways a passive sentence can be avoided in Spanish.

1. by using the **se** construction

The word **se** corresponds to the English *one, they, you,* or *it* used in a general sense as in "*One* should eat when *one* is hungry"or "*They* say he's a nice guy."

To avoid a passive construction, Spanish often uses **se** as a replacement for the passive voice.

*English **is spoken** in many countries.*
Se habla inglés en muchos países.
[word-for-word: *English **speaks** itself in many countries*]

*The office **opens** at 9:00.*
Se abre la oficina a las nueve.
[word-for-word: *the office **opens** itself at nine o'clock*]

2. by using the third person plural of the verb

To avoid the passive construction Spanish often makes *they* (the third person plural) the subject of an active sentence. The "they" corresponds to a general subject such as "*They* say Mexico is very interesting."

*English **is spoken** in many countries.*
Hablan inglés en muchos países.
[word-for-word: ***they speak** English in many countries*]

*The office **opens** at 9:00.*
Abren la oficina a las nueve.
[word-for-word: ***they open** the office at nine o'clock*]

▼▼▼▼▼▼▼▼▼▼▼▼▼▼▼▼▼REVIEW▼▼▼▼▼▼▼▼▼▼▼▼▼▼▼▼▼

Underline the subject in the sentences below.
■ Circle the performer of the action.
■ Identify each sentence as active (A) or passive (P).
■ Identify the tense of the verb: present (P), past (PS), future (F).

1. The cow jumped over the moon.	A P	P PS F
2. The bill was paid by Bob's parents.	A P	P PS F
3. The bank transfers the money.	A P	P PS F
4. Everyone will be going away during August.	A P	P PS F
5. The spring break will be enjoyed by all.	A P	P PS F

30. WHAT IS AN ADJECTIVE?

An **adjective** is a word that describes a noun or a pronoun.

IN ENGLISH
Adjectives are classified according to the way they describe a noun or pronoun.

DESCRIPTIVE ADJECTIVE—A descriptive adjective indicates a quality; it describes what the noun or pronoun is like (see p. 103).

> She read an *interesting* book.
> He has *brown* eyes.

POSSESSIVE ADJECTIVE—A possessive adjective shows possession; it explains to whom something or someone belongs (see p. 106).

> *His* book is lost.
> *Our* parents are away.

INTERROGATIVE ADJECTIVE—An interrogative adjective asks a question about someone or something (see p. 113).

> *Which* parents did you speak to?
> *What* book is lost?

DEMONSTRATIVE ADJECTIVE—A demonstrative adjective points out someone or something (see p. 116).

> *This* teacher is excellent.
> *That* question is very appropriate.

In all these cases it is said that the adjective modifies the noun or pronoun.

IN SPANISH
Adjectives are classified in the same way as in English. The principal difference between English and Spanish adjectives is that in English adjectives generally do not change their form, while in Spanish adjectives agree in gender and number with the noun or pronoun they modify.

31. WHAT IS A DESCRIPTIVE ADJECTIVE?

A **descriptive adjective** is a word that indicates a quality of a noun or pronoun. As the name implies, it *describes* the noun or pronoun.

IN ENGLISH

The descriptive adjective does not change form, regardless of the noun or pronoun it modifies.

> The students are *intelligent.*
> She is an *intelligent* person.

The adjective *intelligent* is the same although the persons described are different in number (*students* is plural and *person* is singular).

Descriptive adjectives are divided into two groups depending on how they are connected to the noun they modify.

A **predicate adjective** is connected to its noun (the subject of the sentence) by a linking verb, usually a form of *to be.*

> The children are *good.*
>   noun   linking predicate adjective
>   subject verb

> The house looks *small.*
>   noun   linking predicate adjective
>   subject verb

An **attributive adjective** is connected directly to its noun and always precedes it.

> The *good* children were praised.
>   attributive noun described
>   adjective

> The family lives in a *small* house.
>   attributive noun described
>   adjective

IN SPANISH

The most important difference between descriptive adjectives in Spanish and English is that in Spanish they change forms. In Spanish, an adjective, predicate and attributive, always agrees with the noun or pronoun it modifies; that is, it must correspond in gender and number to its noun. Thus, before writing an adjective, you will have to determine if the noun or pronoun it modifies is masculine or feminine, singular or plural.

Most adjectives change the final **-o** of the masculine singular form to **-a** to make the feminine form and add **-s** to the masculine or feminine singular form to make it plural.

the red car   el coche **rojo**
                    masc. masc.
                    sing.   sing.

the red table   la mesa **roja**
                    fem.   fem.
                    sing. sing.

the red cars   los coches **rojos**
                    masc. masc.
                    pl.   pl.

the red tables   las mesas **rojas**
                    fem.   fem.
                    pl.   pl.

As you can see in the examples above, in English, the adjective "red" is placed before the noun it modifies, whereas "rojo" is placed after the noun in Spanish. This is not always the case; some Spanish adjectives also come before the noun they modify. Refer to your textbook to learn whether a Spanish adjective is placed before or after the noun it modifies.

Nouns Used as Adjectives

IN ENGLISH

You should be able to recognize nouns used as adjectives; that is, a noun used to modify another noun. When a noun is used to describe another noun, the structure is as follows: the describing noun (adjective) + the noun described.

Spanish is easy.   The *Spanish* class is crowded.
   | |
 noun   adjective describing the noun *class*

Chemistry is difficult.   The *chemistry* books are expensive.
   | |
 noun   adjective describing the noun *books*

IN SPANISH

When a noun is used as an adjective, that is, to describe another noun, the structure is as follows: the noun described + **de** + the describing noun (adjective) without an article. The describing noun remains a noun and does not change its form.

the Spanish class   =   la **clase** de **español**
    | | | |
el español **la clase**   fem.   masc.
       sing.   sing.
                  [word-for-word: *the class of Spanish*]

the chemistry books = los **libros** de **química**
      | | | |
la química **los libros**   masc.   fem.
                   pl.   sing.
                  [word-for-word: *the books of chemistry*]

▼▼▼▼▼▼▼▼▼▼▼▼▼▼▼▼▼▼REVIEW▼▼▼▼▼▼▼▼▼▼▼▼▼▼▼▼▼▼

Circle the adjectives in the sentences below.
- Draw an arrow from the adjective you circled to the noun or pronoun described.

1. The young man was reading a Spanish newspaper.

2. She looked pretty in her red dress.

3. It is interesting.

4. The old piano could still produce good music.

5. Paul was tired after his long walk.

32. WHAT IS A POSSESSIVE ADJECTIVE?

A **possessive adjective** is a word that describes a noun by showing who *possesses* the thing or person being discussed. The owner is called the "possessor" and the noun modified is called the person or thing "possessed."

Whose house is that? It's *my* house.

My is an adjective that tells us who is the possessor of the noun "house."

IN ENGLISH

Here is a list of the possessive adjectives:

Singular

1st person		my
2nd person		your
	masc.	his
3rd person	fem.	her
	neuter	its

Plural

1st person	our
2nd person	your
3rd person	their

Possessive adjectives never change their form, regardless of the thing possessed; they only refer to the possessor.

Is that your house? Yes, it is *my* house.
Are those your keys? Yes, they are *my* keys.

The same possessive adjective *(my)* is used, although the objects possessed are different in number (*house* is singular, *keys* is plural).

What color is John's car? *His* car is blue.
What color is Mary's car? *Her* car is blue.

Although the object possessed is the same *(car),* the possessive adjective is different because the possessor is different *(John* is masculine singular, *Mary* is feminine singular).

IN SPANISH

Like English, a Spanish possessive adjective refers to the possessor, but unlike English, it must agree, like all Spanish adjectives, in gender and number with the noun it modifies, that is, the person or object possessed.

For example, in the phrase **nuestro hermano** (*our brother*) the first letters of the possessive adjective **nuestr-** refer to the first person plural possessor *our*, while the ending **-o** is masculine singular to agree with **hermano** which is masculine singular. Let us see what happens when we make the noun *brother* plural.

> We love **our brothers**.
> Queremos a nuestros hermanos.
>
> masc. pl. endings
> 1st pers. pl.
> possessor

> **Nuestros** refers to the possessor *(our)*, but agrees in gender and number with the noun **hermanos.**

Spanish has two sets of possessive adjectives: the stressed and the unstressed. The short, unstressed forms are the most common and will be considered first.

Unstressed Possessive Adjectives

Let us look at the unstressed Spanish possessive adjectives to see how they are formed.

MY, YOUR (fam. sing.) **HIS, HER, YOUR** (form. sing.), **THEIR**, and **YOUR** (form. pl.)

In Spanish, each of these possessive adjectives has two forms depending on the number of the noun possessed: 1. the singular (the same for both genders), and 2. the plural (the same for both genders).

Here are the steps you should follow in choosing the correct possessive adjective.

1. Indicate the possessor. This is shown by the two letters of the possessive adjective.

my	**mi**
your (fam. sing.)	**tu**
his	
her	
your (form. sing.)	**su**
their	
your (form. pl.)	

2. Choose the ending according to the number of the noun possessed.

- noun is singular → the form of the possessive adjective does not change

    | Ana lee **mi** libro. | *Ana reads **my** book.* |
    | Ana lee **tu** libro. | *Ana reads **your** book.* |
    | Ana lee **su** libro. | *Ana reads **(her, your, their)** book.* |

- noun is plural → add **-s** to the possessive adjective

    | Ana lee **mis** libros. | *Ana reads **my** books.* |
    | Ana lee **tus** libros. | *Ana reads **your** books.* |
    | Ana lee **sus** libros. | *Ana reads **his** (her, your, their) books.* |

Since the word **su** has many possible English meanings, Spanish speakers often replace it with the phrase: noun + **de** + prepositional pronoun.

his book			el libro **de él**
her book			el libro **de ella**
your (form. sing.) *book*	} **su** libro {	el libro **de Ud.**
their book			el libro **de ellos (ellas)**
your (form. pl.) *book*			el libro **de Uds.**

OUR, YOUR (fam. pl.)

In Spanish, these possessive adjectives have four forms depending on the gender and number of the noun possessed: 1. the masculine singular; 2. the feminine singular; 3. the masculine plural; 4. the feminine plural.

Here are the steps you should follow in choosing the correct possessive adjective.

1. Indicate the possessor. This is shown by the first letters of the possessive adjective.

    | our | **nuestr-** |
    | your (fam. pl.) | **vuestr-** |

2. Choose the ending according to the gender and number of the noun possessed. Place the unstressed possessive adjective before the noun.

- noun possessed is masculine singular → add **-o**

    Ana lee **nuestro** libro.   *Ana reads **our** book.*
    masc. sing.

    Ana lee **vuestro** libro.   *Ana reads **your** book.*

- noun possessed is feminine singular → add **-a**

  Ana lee **nuestra** revista. *Ana reads **our** magazine.*
  fem. sing.

  Ana lee **vuestra** revista. *Ana reads **your** magazine.*

- noun possessed is masculine plural → add **-os**

  Ana lee **nuestros** libros. *Ana reads **our** books.*
  masc. pl.

  Ana lee **vuestros** libros. *Ana reads **your** books.*

- noun possessed is feminine plural → add **-as**

  Ana lee **nuestras** revistas. *Ana reads **our** magazines.*
  fem. pl.

  Ana lee **vuestras** revistas. *Ana reads **your** magazines.*

Careful

In Spanish and in English, the subject and the possessive adjective do not necessarily match. It all depends on what you want to say.

¿Tienes **tu** libro? *Do **you** have **your** book?*
2nd pers. sing. 2nd pers. sing.

¿Tienes **mi** libro? *Do **you** have **my** book?*
2nd pers. 1st pers. 2nd pers. 1st pers.
sing. sing. sing. sing.

Before you write a sentence with *your,* decide whether it is appropriate to use the familiar or formal forms in Spanish. Then, make sure that all the forms, including the verb, correspond.

You are reading *your* letter.
{
Tú lees **tu** carta.
Ud. lee **su** carta.
Vosotros leéis **vuestra** carta.
Uds. leen **su** carta.
}

Stressed Possessive Adjectives

Spanish also has another set of possessive adjectives called **stressed possessive adjectives**; they follow the noun they modify. They are used to add emphasis to the possessor and correspond to the English "of mine," "of yours," etc.

> that dress *of mine* [instead of *my* dress]
> those books *of yours* [instead of *your* books]

The use of these stressed forms is more common in Spanish than in English.

Like the unstressed possessives the first letters of the stressed possessive adjective refer to the possessor and the ending agrees with the item or person possessed. For example, in the phrase **el libro tuyo** (*your book*) the first letters of the possessive adjective **tuy-** refer to a 2nd person singular possessor *your;* the ending **-o** is masculine singular to agree with **libro** which is masculine singular.

Here is a list of the stressed possessive adjectives used with a masculine singular noun.

mío	*mine; of mine*
tuyo	*your; of yours*
suyo	*his, her, your; of his, of hers, of yours*
nuestro	*our; of ours*
vuestro	*your; of yours*
suyo	*their, your; of theirs, of yours*

Here are the steps you should follow in choosing the correct stressed possessive adjective.

1. Indicate the possessor. This is shown by the first letters of the possessive adjective.

mine, of mine	**mí-**
your, of yours (fam. sing.)	**tuy-**
his, of his her, of hers your, of yours (form. sing.)	**suy-**
our, of ours	**nuestr-**
your, of yours (fam. pl.)	**vuestr-**
their, of theirs your, of yours (form. pl.)	**suy-**

2. Choose the ending according to the gender and number of the noun possessed. Place the stressed possessive adjective after the noun.

- noun possessed is masculine singular → add **-o**

  Ana lee un libro **mío**.   *Ana is reading a book of mine.*

  masc. sing.

- noun possessed is feminine singular → add **-a**

  Ana lee una revista **mía**.   *Ana is reading a magazine of mine.*

  fem. sing.

- noun possessed is masculine plural → add **-os**

  Ana lee unos libros **míos**. *Ana is reading some books of mine.*

  masc. pl.

- noun possessed is feminine plural → add **-as**

  Ana lee unas revistas **mías**. *Ana is reading some magazines of mine.*

  fem. pl.

Here are two other examples.

This car is John's. My car is in the garage.
1. POSSESSOR: 1st person singular
2. GENDER AND NUMBER OF NOUN POSSESSED:
   El coche *(car)* is masculine singular.

El coche **mío** está en el garaje.

masc. sing.

These chairs of yours are very comfortable.
1. POSSESSOR: 2nd person singular
2. GENDER AND NUMBER OF NOUN POSSESSED:
   Las sillas *(chairs)* are feminine plural.

Estas sillas **tuyas** son muy cómodas.

fem. pl.

▼▼▼▼▼▼▼▼▼▼▼▼▼▼▼▼▼▼REVIEW▼▼▼▼▼▼▼▼▼▼▼▼▼▼▼▼▼▼

Circle the possessive adjectives in the sentences below.

- Draw an arrow from the possessive adjective to the noun it modifies.
- Circle the number of the possessive adjective: singular (S) or plural (P).
- Using the charts in this section, fill in the Spanish unstressed possessive adjective in the Spanish sentences below.

1. I put my book on the desk.

   NOUN MODIFIED IN SPANISH: masculine   S   P

   Puse _____ libro sobre el escritorio.

2. Mary is wearing your (familiar) boots.

   NOUN MODIFIED IN SPANISH: feminine   S   P

   María lleva _____ botas.

3. Roberto is looking for his mother.

   NOUN MODIFIED IN SPANISH: feminine   S   P

   Roberto busca a _____ madre.

4. Our children are very young.

   NOUN MODIFIED IN SPANISH: masculine   S   P

   _____ hijos son muy jóvenes.

33. WHAT IS AN INTERROGATIVE ADJECTIVE?

An **interrogative adjective** is a word that asks a question about a noun.

IN ENGLISH
The words *which* and *what* are called interrogative adjectives when they come in front of a noun and are used to ask a question about that noun.

> *Which* instructor is teaching the course?
> *What* courses are you taking?

IN SPANISH
There are two interrogative adjectives: **qué** which corresponds to the English *which* or *what* and the forms of **cuánto** meaning *how much* or *how many*.[1]

1. to say "which book" or "what dress" in Spanish, you use the following structure: *which* or *what* + noun → **qué** + noun

   Qué is invariable; that is, it does not change form to agree in number and gender with the noun it modifies.

   > ¿**Qué** revista lees?
   > *What magazine are you reading?*

   > ¿**Qué** libros quieres?
   > *Which books do you want?*

2. to ask "how many students" or "how much time" in Spanish, you use the following structure: *how much* or *how many* + noun → **cuánto** + noun

   Cuánto has four forms to agree in gender and number with the noun it modifies.

   > *How much money do you need?*

   > **El dinero** *(money)* is masculine singular
   > so the word for "how much" must be masculine singular.

   > ¿**Cuánto** dinero necesitas?
   >   ⌐—┬—⌐
   >   masc. sing.

---

[1]In certain areas of the Spanish-speaking world **cuál** and **cuáles** can function as interrogative adjectives: ¿**Cuál libro quieres?** *(Which book do you want?)*. However, **qué** is the interrogative adjective *which/what* used in standard Spanish.

How much soup do you want?
>   **La sopa** *(soup)* is feminine singular
>   so the word for "how much" must be feminine singular.

¿**Cuánta** sopa quieres?
>   fem. sing.

How many records do you have?
>   **Los discos** *(records)* is masculine plural
>   so the word for "how many" must be masculine plural.

¿**Cuántos** discos tienes?
>   masc. pl.

How many suitcases are you bringing?
>   **Las maletas** *(suitcases)* is feminine plural
>   so the word for "how many" must be feminine plural.

¿**Cuántas** maletas traes?
>   fem. pl.

Careful

The word "what" is not always an interrogative adjective. It can also be an interrogative pronoun. When it is a pronoun, *what* (**qué**) is not followed by a noun.

What is on the table?
>   interrogative pronoun

¿**Qué** hay en la mesa?

The expression "how many" is not always an interrogative adjective. It can also be an interrogative pronoun. When it is a pronoun, *how many* (**cuánto**) is not followed by a noun.

How many do you need?
>   interrogative pronoun

¿**Cuántos** necesitas?

It is important to distinguish interrogative adjectives from interrogative pronouns because sometimes different words are used in Spanish (see **What is an Interrogative Pronoun?**, p. 153).

▼▼▼▼▼▼▼▼▼▼▼▼▼▼▼▼REVIEW▼▼▼▼▼▼▼▼▼▼▼▼▼▼▼▼

I. Circle the interrogative adjectives in the sentences below.
- Draw an arrow from the interrogative adjective to the noun it modifies.

1. Which book is yours?

2. Please tell me what exercises are due tomorrow.

3. Which house do you live in?

II. Circle the interrogative adjectives in the sentences below.
- Draw an arrow from the interrogative adjective to the noun it modifies.
- Indicate if the noun modifies is singular (S) or plural (P).
- Fill in the Spanish interrogative adjective in the Spanish sentences below.

1. How many shirts did you buy?

NOUN MODIFIED IN SPANISH: feminine   S   P

¿ _____ camisas compraste?

2. How much wine are you bringing to the party?

NOUN MODIFIED IN SPANISH: masculine   S   P

¿_____ vino traes a la fiesta?

3. How many telephones are there in your house?

NOUN MODIFIED IN SPANISH: masculine   S   P

¿ _____ teléfonos hay en tu casa?

4. How much salad do you want?

NOUN MODIFIED IN SPANISH: feminine   S   P

¿ _____ ensalada quieres?

34. WHAT IS A DEMONSTRATIVE ADJECTIVE?

A **demonstrative adjective** is a word used to point out a person or an object.

IN ENGLISH

The demonstrative adjectives are *this* and *that* in the singular and *these* and *those* in the plural. They are rare examples of adjectives that agree in number with the noun they modify; *this* changes to *these* and *that* changes to *those* when they modify a plural noun.

Singular	Plural
this cat	*these* cats
that man	*those* men

This and *these* refer to a person or object near the speaker, and *that* and *those* refer to a person or object away from the speaker.

IN SPANISH

There are three sets of demonstrative adjectives that change to agree in gender and number with the nouns they modify. In order to say *"this* house" or *"that* room" you start by determining where the person or object is in relation to the speaker or the person spoken to. Then, determine the gender and number of the noun you wish to point out and make the demonstrative adjective agree with that noun.

1. noun near the speaker: *this, these* → a form of **este**

   ▪ noun modified is masculine singular → **este**

   > **Este** cuarto es grande.
   >> **Cuarto** *(room)* is masculine singular,
   >> so the word for *this* must be masculine singular.
   >
   > *This room is large.*

   ▪ noun modified is feminine singular → **esta**

   > **Esta** casa es grande.
   >> **Casa** *(house)* is feminine singular,
   >> so the word for *this* must be feminine singular.
   >
   > *This house is large.*

   ▪ noun modified is masculine plural → **estos**

   > **Estos** cuartos son grandes.
   >> **Cuartos** *(rooms)* is masculine plural,
   >> so the word for *these* must be masculine plural.
   >
   > *These rooms are large.*

■ noun modified is feminine plural → **estas**

> **Estas** casas son grandes.
>> **Casas** *(houses)* is feminine plural,
>> so the word for *these* must be feminine plural.
>
> *These houses are large.*

2. noun near the person spoken to: that, those → a form of **ese**

■ noun modified is masculine singular → **ese**

> **Ese** cuarto es grande.
>> **Cuarto** *(room)* is masculine singular,
>> so the word for *that* must be masculine singular.
>
> *That room is large.*

■ noun modified is feminine singular → **esa**

> **Esa** casa es grande.
>> **Casa** *(house)* is feminine singular,
>> so the word for *that* must be feminine singular.
>
> *That house is large.*

■ noun modified is masculine plural → **esos**

> **Esos** cuartos son grandes.
>> **Cuartos** *(rooms)* is masculine plural,
>> so the word for *those* must be masculine plural.
>
> *Those rooms are large.*

■ noun modified is feminine plural → **esas**

> **Estas** casas son grandes.
>> **Casas** *(houses)* is feminine plural,
>> so the word for *those* must be feminine plural.
>
> *Those houses are large.*

3. nouns away from both the speaker and the person spoken to: *that, those* → a form of **aquel**

Since English does not have this third set of demonstrative adjectives, there is no good translation for them. Sometimes the forms of **aquel** translate as "that, those over there" to imply the distance.

■ noun modified is masculine singular → **aquel**

> **Aquel** cuarto es grande.
>> **Cuarto** *(room)* is masculine singular,
>> so the word for *that* must be masculine singular.
>
> *That room (over there) is large.*

■ noun modified is feminine singular → **aquella**

> **Aquella** casa es grande.
> > **Casa** *(house)* is feminine singular,
> > so the word for *that* must be feminine singular.
>
> *That house (over there) is large.*

■ noun modified is masculine plural → **aquellos**

> **Aquellos** cuartos son grandes.
> > **Cuartos** *(rooms)* is masculine plural,
> > so the word for *those* must be masculine plural.
>
> *Those rooms (over there) are large.*

■ noun modified is feminine plural → **aquellas**

> **Aquellas** casas son grandes.
> > **Casas** *(houses)* is feminine plural,
> > so the word for *those* must be feminine plural.
>
> *Those houses (over there) are large.*

Careful

The three sets of demonstrative adjectives may also function as demonstrative pronouns. As demonstrative pronouns they are not followed by a noun and they carry a written accent. (See **What is a Demonstrative Pronoun?**, p. 160.)

▼▼▼▼▼▼▼▼▼▼▼▼▼▼▼▼REVIEW▼▼▼▼▼▼▼▼▼▼▼▼▼▼▼▼

Circle the demonstrative adjectives in the sentences below.
- Draw an arrow from the demonstrative adjective to the noun it modifies.
- Indicate if the noun modified is singular (S) or plural (P).
- Fill in the Spanish demonstrative adjective in the Spanish sentences.

1. They prefer that restaurant.

   NOUN MODIFIED IN SPANISH: masculine   S   P

   Prefieren _____ restaurante.

2. Those houses over there are very expensive.

   NOUN MODIFIED IN SPANISH: feminine   S   P

   _____ casas son muy caras.

3. I bought these shoes in Spain.

   NOUN MODIFIED IN SPANISH: masculine   S   P

   Compré _____ zapatos en España.

4. Do you want this magazine?

   NOUN MODIFIED IN SPANISH: feminine   S   P

   ¿Quieres _____ revista?

35. WHAT IS MEANT BY COMPARISON OF ADJECTIVES?

We compare adjectives when two or more nouns have the same quality (height, size, color, any characteristic) and we want to indicate that one of these nouns has a greater, lesser, or equal degree of this quality.[1]

comparison of adjectives

Paul is *tall* but Mary is *taller.*

adjective
modifies *Paul*

adjective
modifies *Mary*

In both English and Spanish there are two types of comparison: comparative and superlative.

Comparative

The **comparative** is used to compare one noun to another noun. There are three degrees of comparison.

IN ENGLISH

GREATER DEGREE—The comparison of greater degree (more) is formed differently depending on the length of the adjective being compared.

- short adjective + *-er* + *than*

    Paul is *taller than* Mary.
    Susan is *older than* her sister.

- *more* + longer adjective + *than*

    Mary is *more intelligent than* John.
    My car is *more expensive than* your car.

LESSER DEGREE—The comparison of lesser degree (less) is formed as follows: *not as* + adjective + *as*, or *less* + adjective + *than*

    Your car is *not as expensive as* my car.
    John is *less intelligent than* Mary.

EQUAL DEGREE—The comparison of equal degree (same) is formed as follows: *as* + adjective + *as*

    Robert is *as intelligent as* Mary.
    My car is *as expensive as* his car.

---

[1]In English and in Spanish, the structure for comparing adverbs (see **What is an Adverb?**, p. 124) is the same as the structure for comparing adjectives.

IN SPANISH

There are the same three degrees of comparison of adjectives as in English. Remember that agreement between the adjective and noun is always required. However, since a comparative adjective always describes more than one noun, it always agrees in gender and number with the subject.

GREATER DEGREE—The comparative of greater degree is formed as follows: **más** *(more)* + adjective + **que** *(than)*.

María es **más alta que** Roberto.
            |
      agrees with **María**
*Mary is **taller than** Robert.*

LESSER DEGREE—The comparison of lesser degree is formed as follows: **menos** *(less)* + adjective + **que** *(than)*.

Roberto es **menos alto que** María.
            |
      agrees with **Roberto**
*Robert is **less tall than** Mary.*

EQUAL DEGREE—The comparative of equal qualities is formed as follows: **tan** *(as)* + adjective + **como** *(as)*.

María es **tan alta como** Juan.
*Mary is **as tall as** John.*

Superlative

The **superlative** is used to compare one noun to at least two other nouns. There are two degrees of superlative.

IN ENGLISH

HIGHEST DEGREE—The superlative of highest degree is formed differently depending on the length of the adjectives:

- *the* + short adjective + *-est*

    Mary is *the smartest.*
    My car is *the cheapest* on the market.

- *the most* + long adjective

    Mary is *the most intelligent.*
    His car is *the most expensive* of all.

LOWEST DEGREE—The superlative of lowest degree degree is formed as follows: *the least* + adjective.

> Paul is *the least active*.
> Your car is *the least expensive* of all.

IN SPANISH

There are the same two degrees of the superlative.

HIGHEST DEGREE—The superlative of highest degree is formed by **el, la, los, las** (depending on the gender and number of the noun described) + **más** *(most)* + adjective.

> Juan es **el más bajo** de la familia.
> masc. sing.
>
> *John is **the shortest** in the family.*

> María es **la más alta**.
> fem. sing.
>
> *Mary is **the tallest**.*

> Carlos y Roberto son **los más divertidos** de la clase.
> masc. pl.
>
> *Charles and Robert are **the funniest** in the class.*

> Teresa y Gloria son **las más inteligentes**.
> fem. pl.
>
> *Teresa and Gloria are **the most intelligent**.*

LOWEST DEGREE—The superlative of lowest degree is formed by **el, la, los, las** (depending on the gender and number of the noun described) + **menos** *(least)* + adjective.

> Mi coche es **el menos caro**.
> masc. sing.
>
> *My car is **the least expensive**.*

Careful

In English and in Spanish, a few adjectives have irregular forms of comparison which you will have to memorize individually.

adjective   Esta manzana es **buena**.
                   *This apple is **good**.*

comparative   Esta manzana es **mejor**.
                   *This apple is **better**.*

superlative   Esta manzana es **la mejor**.
                   *This apple is **the best**.*

▼▼▼▼▼▼▼▼▼▼▼▼▼▼▼▼▼REVIEW▼▼▼▼▼▼▼▼▼▼▼▼▼▼▼▼▼▼

Underline the comparative and superlative adjectives in the sentences below.
- Draw an arrow from the adjective to the noun it modifies.
- Indicate the various degrees of comparison: superlative (S); comparative of greater degree (C+); comparative of equal degree (C=); or comparative of lesser degree (C-).

1. The teacher is older than the students.	S	C+	C=	C-
2. He is less intelligent than I am.	S	C+	C=	C-
3. Mary is as tall as Paul.	S	C+	C=	C-
4. That boy is the worst in the school.	S	C+	C=	C-
5. Paul is a better student than Mary.	S	C+	C=	C-

36. WHAT IS AN ADVERB?

An **adverb** is a word that describes a verb, an adjective, or another adverb.[1]

Mary drives *well*.
| |
verb   adverb

The house is *very* big.
| |
adverb adjective

The girl ran *too quickly*.
| |
adverb adverb

IN ENGLISH

There are different types of adverbs:

- adverbs of manner answer the question *how*? They are the most common adverbs and can usually be recognized by their **-ly** ending.

    Mary sings *beautifully*.
    Beautifully describes the verb *sings*, how Mary sings.

    They parked the car *carefully*.
    Carefully describes the verb *parked*, how the car was parked.

- adverbs of quantity or degree answer the question *how much?*

    Paul does *well enough* in class.

- adverbs of time answer the question *when?*

    He will be home *soon*.

- adverbs of place answer the question *where?*

    The old were left *behind*.

IN SPANISH

Adverbs must be memorized as vocabulary. Most adverbs of manner can be recognized by their ending **-mente** which corresponds to the English ending -*ly*.

natural**mente**	*naturally*
general**mente**	*generally*
rápida**mente**	*rapidly*

---

[1] In English and in Spanish, the structure for comparing adverbs is the same as the structure for comparing adjectives (see **What is Meant by Comparison of Adjectives?**, p. 120).

The most important fact for you to remember is that adverbs are invariable; this means that they never become plural, nor do they have gender.

Adverb or Adjective?

Because adverbs are invariable and Spanish adjectives must agree with the noun they modify, you must be able to distinguish one from the other. When you write a sentence in Spanish, always make sure that adjectives agree with the nouns or pronouns they modify and that adverbs remain unchanged.

*The **tall** girl talked **rapidly**.*

> *Tall* modifies the noun *girl*; it is an adjective. *Rapidly* modifies the verb *talked*; it describes how she talked; it is an adverb.

La chica **alta** habló **rápidamente**.

     fem. sing.   adverb

*The **tall** boy talked **rapidly**.*

> *Tall* modifies the noun *boy*; it is an adjective. *Rapidly* modifies the verb *talked*; it describes how he talked; it is an adverb.

El chico **alto** habló **rápidamente**.

     masc. sing.   adverb

Remember that in English *good* is an adjective; *well* is an adverb.

The boy writes *good* English.

> *Good* modifies the noun *English;* it is therefore an adjective.

The student writes *well.*

> *Well* modifies the verb *writes;* it is therefore an adverb.

Likewise, in Spanish **bueno** is an adjective meaning *good;* **bien** is the adverb meaning *well.*

*The **good** students speak Spanish **well**.*

  adjective   adverb

Los estudiantes **buenos** hablan español **bien**.

      masc. pl.   adverb

▼▼▼▼▼▼▼▼▼▼▼▼▼▼▼▼▼▼REVIEW▼▼▼▼▼▼▼▼▼▼▼▼▼▼▼▼▼▼

Circle the adverbs in the sentences below.

■ Draw an arrow from the adverb to the word it modifies.

1. The students arrived early.

2. Paul learned the lesson really quickly.

3. The students were too tired to study.

4. He has a reasonably secure income.

5. Mary is a good student who speaks Spanish very well.

37. WHAT IS A CONJUNCTION?

A **conjunction** is a word that links words or groups of words.

IN ENGLISH

There are two kinds of conjunctions: coordinating and subordinating.

Coordinating conjunctions join words, phrases, and clauses that are equal; they coordinate elements of equal rank. The major coordinating conjunctions are *and, but, or, nor, for,* and *yet.*

> good *or* evil
> over the river *and* through the woods
> They invited us, *but* we couldn't go.

Subordinating conjunctions join a dependent clause to a main clause; they subordinate one clause to another. A clause introduced by a subordinating conjunction is called a **subordinate clause**. Typical subordinating conjunctions are *before, after, since, although, because, if, unless, so that, while, that,* and *when.*

> *Although* we were invited, we didn't go.
> subordinating   main
> conjunction   clause

> They left *because* they were bored.
>   main   subordinating
>   clause   conjunction

> He said *that* he was tired.
>   main   subordinating
>   clause conjunction

Notice that the subordinate clause may come either at the beginning of the sentence or after the main clause.

IN SPANISH

Conjunctions must be memorized as vocabulary.

Remember that, like adverbs and prepositions, conjunctions are invariable; that is, they never change their form.

▼▼▼▼▼▼▼▼▼▼▼▼▼▼▼▼▼REVIEW▼▼▼▼▼▼▼▼▼▼▼▼▼▼▼▼▼

Circle the coordinating and subordinating conjunctions in the sentences below.
- Underline the words each conjunction serves to coordinate or to subordinate.

1. Mary and Paul were going to study French or Spanish.

2. She did not study because she was too tired.

3. Not only had he forgotten his ticket, but he had forgotten his passport as well.

38. WHAT IS A PREPOSITION?

A **preposition** is a word that shows the relationship of one word (usually a noun or pronoun) to another word in the sentence. The noun or pronoun following the preposition is called the **object of the preposition**. The preposition plus its object is called a **prepositional phrase**.

IN ENGLISH
Prepositions normally indicate position, direction, or time.

- prepositions showing position

> Paul was *in* the car.
> Mary put the books *on* the table.

- prepositions showing direction

> Mary went *to* school.
> The students came directly *from* class.

- prepositions showing time

> Spanish people go on vacation *in* August.
> *Before* class, they went to eat.

Not all prepositions are single words:

because of	in front of	instead of
due to	in spite of	on account of

IN SPANISH
You will have to memorize prepositions as vocabulary. Their meaning and use must be studied carefully. There are three important things to remember:

1. Prepositions are invariable. This means they never change their form. (They never become plural, nor do they have a gender.)

2. Prepositions are tricky. Every language uses prepositions differently. Do not assume that the same preposition is used in Spanish as in English, or even that a preposition will be used in Spanish when you must use one in English (and vice versa).

> ENGLISH → SPANISH
> **change of prepositions**
> to laugh *at*   reirse **de** *(of)*
> to consist *of*   consistir **en** *(in)*

ENGLISH	→	SPANISH
preposition		**no preposition**
to look *for*		buscar
to look *at*		mirar
no preposition		**preposition**
to leave		salir **de**
to enter		entrar **en**

A dictionary will usually give you the verb plus the preposition when one is required.

3. Although the position of a preposition in an English sentence may vary, it cannot vary in Spanish. Spoken English often places a preposition at the end of the sentence; in this position it is called a **dangling preposition**. In formal English there is a strong tendency to avoid dangling prepositions by placing them within the sentence or at the beginning of a question.

Spoken English	→	**Formal English**
The man I spoke *to* is Spanish.		The man *to* whom I spoke is Spanish.
Who are you playing *with*?		*With* whom are you playing?
Here is the girl you asked *about*.		Here is the girl *about* whom you asked.

Spanish places prepositions the same way as formal English; that is, within the sentence or at the beginning of a question. A preposition cannot be placed at the end of a Spanish sentence.

Roberto es el hombre **a** quien le hablé ayer.
Roberto is the man to whom I spoke yesterday.

¿**Con** quién juegas?
With whom are you playing?

There are some English expressions where the natural position of the preposition is at the end of the sentence; it is not a question of the difference in spoken or formal language.

What are you thinking *about*?

Changing the structure by placing the preposition within the sentence would sound awkward.

About what are you thinking?

However, as awkward as it may sound in English, this is the structure that must be used in the Spanish sentence.

¿**En qué** piensas?

Careful
Do not translate an English verb + preposition with a word-for-word equivalent (see pp. 21-22).

▼▼▼▼▼▼▼▼▼▼▼▼▼▼▼▼REVIEW▼▼▼▼▼▼▼▼▼▼▼▼▼▼▼▼

Circle the prepositions in the following sentences.

1. The students didn't understand what the lesson was about.

2. The professor had come from Peru by boat.

3. The teacher walked around the room as she talked.

4. Contrary to popular opinion he was a good student.

5. The garden between the two houses was very small.

39. WHAT ARE OBJECTS?

Every sentence consists, at the very least, of a subject and a verb. This is called the **sentence base**.

Children play.
Work stopped.

The subject of the sentence is usually a noun or pronoun. Many sentences contain other nouns or pronouns that are related to the action of the verb or to a preposition. These nouns or pronouns are called **objects**.

Paul writes a letter.
subject | object
verb

He speaks to Mary.
subject | object
verb

Paul goes out with her sister.
subject | object
verb

There are three types of objects: direct object, indirect object, and object of a preposition.

Direct Object

IN ENGLISH

A **direct object** is a noun or pronoun that receives the action of the verb directly, without a preposition between the verb and the following noun or pronoun. It answers the question *what?* or *whom?* asked after the verb.[1]

Paul writes *a letter*.
QUESTION: Paul writes what? ANSWER: A letter.
A letter is the direct object.

They see *Paul and Mary*.
QUESTION: They see whom? ANSWER: Paul and Mary.
Paul and Mary are the two direct objects.

---

[1] In this section, we will consider active sentences only. (See **What is Meant by Active and Passive Voice?**, p. 97.)

Do not assume thay any word that comes right after a verb is automatically the direct object. It must answer the question *what?* or *whom?*

> Paul sees well.
>> QUESTION: Paul see what? ANSWER: No answer.
>> QUESTION: Paul see whom? ANSWER: No answer.

There is no direct object in the sentence. *Well* is an adverb; it answers the question: Paul sees *how?*

Verbs can be classified as to whether or not they take a direct object.

■ **a transitive verb** is a verb that takes a direct object

> The boy threw the *ball.*
>> |
>> direct object

■ an **intransitive verb** is a verb that does not require a direct object

> Paul *is sleeping.*
>> |
>> intransitive verb

IN SPANISH

As in English, a direct object is a noun or pronoun that receives the action of the verb directly. It answers the one-word question *what?* or *whom?* asked after the verb.

> Pablo escribe **una carta**.
>> QUESTION: Paul writes *what?* ANSWER: A letter.
>> **Una carta** *(a letter)* is the direct object.
>
> *Paul writes a letter.*

In Spanish when the direct object of the verb is a person, it is preceded by the word **a**. This is called the **personal a**. It does not have an English translation.

> Juan ve **a las muchachas**.
>> Personal **a** followed by a direct object noun referring to persons.
>
> *John sees the girls.*

> Juan ve **al hombre**.
>> |
>> a + el
>> Personal **a** followed by a direct object noun referring to a person.
>
> *John sees the man.*

Juan ve **la casa**.

Direct object noun referring to a thing; no personal **a** included.

*John sees **the house**.*

Indirect Object

IN ENGLISH

An **indirect object** is a noun or pronoun that receives the action of the verb indirectly. It answers the two-word question *to whom?* or *to what?* asked after the verb.

John writes *his brother*.

QUESTION: John writes to whom? ANSWER: To his brother.
His brother is the indirect object.

Sometimes the word *to* is included in the English sentence.[1]

John speaks *to Paul and Mary*.

QUESTION: John speaks to whom? ANSWER: To Paul and Mary.
Paul and Mary are the two indirect objects.

IN SPANISH

As in English, an indirect object is a noun or pronoun that receives the action of the verb indirectly. It answers the two-word question *to whom?* or *to what?* asked after the verb. The English word *to* is expressed by **a** in Spanish. The indirect object pronouns **le** or **les** must always be used even though the indirect object noun is also included in the sentence. **Le** is used when the indirect object noun is singular and **les** is used when the indirect object noun is plural (see **What is an Object Pronoun?**, p. 139).

Juan **le** escribe **a su hermano**.
⎣_____⊤_____⎦
      singular
*John writes **(to) his brother**.*

Juan **les** habla **a Pablo y a María**.
⎣_____⊤_____⎦
       plural
*John speaks **to Paul and Mary**.*

---

[1]In English "to Paul and Mary" is called a **prepositional phrase** because it is a phrase that begins with the preposition *to*; in this book we refer to phrases like "to Paul and Mary" as indirect objects since that is how they function in Spanish.

Sentences With a Direct and Indirect Object

A sentence may contain both a direct object and an indirect object.

IN ENGLISH
When a sentence has both a direct and indirect object, the following two word orders are possible:

1. subject (s) + verb (v) + indirect object (IO) + direct object (DO)

> Paul gave his sister a gift.
> | | | |
>   S   V   IO   DO

> QUESTION: Who gave a gift? ANSWER: Paul.
> *Paul* is the subject.

> QUESTION: Paul gave what? ANSWER: A gift.
> *A gift* is the direct object.

> QUESTION: Paul gave a gift to whom? ANSWER: His sister.
> *His sister* is the indirect object.

2. subject + verb + direct object + *to* + indirect object

> Paul gave a gift to his sister.
> | | | | |
>   S   V   DO *to*   IO

The first structure, under #1, is the most common. However, because there is no "to" preceding the indirect object, it is more difficult to identify its function than in the second structure. Be sure to ask the questions to establish the function of words in a sentence.

IN SPANISH
When a sentence contains both a direct and an indirect object noun, there is only one word order possible: subject + **le / les** + verb + direct object + **a** + indirect object

> Pablo le escribe **una carta a su hermano.**
> | | | | | |
>   S **le** V   DO **a**   IO
> *Paul writes **his brother a letter**.*
> *Paul writes **a letter to his brother**.*

Notice that the direct object noun precedes the indirect object noun.

Object of a Preposition

IN ENGLISH

An **object of a preposition** is a noun or pronoun that follows a preposition and is related to it. It answers the question *what?* or *whom?* asked after the preposition.

> Paul is leaving *with Mary*.
>> QUESTION: Paul is leaving with whom? ANSWER: With Mary.
>> *Mary* is the object of the preposition *with*.
>
> He works *for Mr. Jones*.
>> QUESTION: He works for whom? ANSWER: For Mr. Jones.
>> *Mr. Jones* is the object of the preposition *for*.

IN SPANISH

As in English an object of a preposition is a noun or pronoun that follows a preposition and is related to it.

> Pablo sale **con María**.
> *Paul is leaving **with Mary***.
>
> Trabaja **para el Sr. Jones**.
> *He works **for Mr. Jones***.

Careful

The relationship between verb and object are often different in English and Spanish. For example, a verb may take an object of a preposition in English but a direct object in Spanish. For this reason, it is important that you pay close attention to such differences when you learn Spanish verbs. Your textbook, as well as dictionaries, will indicate when a Spanish verb is followed by a preposition.

Here are some examples of the kinds of differences you are most likely to encounter.

Object of a preposition in English → **Direct object in Spanish**

> *I am looking **for the book***.
>> FUNCTION IN ENGLISH: object of a preposition
>> QUESTION: I am looking for what? ANSWER: The book.
>> *The book* is the object of the preposition *for*.
>
> Busco **el libro**.
>> FUNCTION IN SPANISH: direct object
>> QUESTION: ¿Qué busco? ANSWER: El libro.
>> Since **buscar** is not followed by a preposition, it takes a direct object.

Many common verbs require an object of a preposition in English but a direct object in Spanish.

to look for	buscar
to look at	mirar
to ask for	pedir
to listen to	escuchar
to wait for	esperar
to wait on	servir

Direct object in English → **Object of a preposition in Spanish**

*John remembers **his apartment** in Madrid.*
FUNCTION IN ENGLISH: direct object
QUESTION: John remembers what? ANSWER: His apartment.
His apartment is the direct object.

Juan se acuerda **de su apartamento** en Madrid.
FUNCTION IN SPANISH: object of a preposition
QUESTION: ¿De qué se acuerda Juan? ANSWER: De su apartamento.
The verb is **acordarse de**; it requires an object for the preposition **de**.

A few common verbs require a direct object in English but an object of a preposition in Spanish.

to enjoy	gozar **de**
to enter	entrar **en**
to forget	olvidarse **de**
to leave	salir **de**
to marry	casarse **con**
to play	jugar **a**
to remember	acordarse **de**

Always identify the function of a word within the language in which you are working; do not mix English and Spanish patterns.

Summary

The different types of objects in a sentence can be identified by looking to see if they are introduced by a preposition and, if so, by which one.

DIRECT OBJECT—An object that receives the action of the verb directly, without a preposition.

INDIRECT OBJECT—An object that receives the action of the verb indirectly, sometimes with the preposition *to*.

OBJECT OF A PREPOSITION—An object that receives the action of the verb through a preposition.

Your ability to recognize the three kinds of objects is essential. With pronouns, for instance, a different Spanish pronoun is used for the English pronoun *him* depending on whether *him* is a direct object (**lo**), an indirect object (**le**), or an object of a preposition (**él**).

▼▼▼▼▼▼▼▼▼▼▼▼▼▼▼▼▼REVIEW▼▼▼▼▼▼▼▼▼▼▼▼▼▼▼▼▼

Next to Q, write the question you need to ask to find the object.
- Next to A, write the answer to the question you just asked.
- In the column to the right, identify the kind of object it is: direct object (DO), indirect object (IO), or object of a preposition (OP).

1. The children took a shower.

Q: _____

A: _____   DO   IO   OP

2. They ate the meal in the restaurant.

Q: _____

A: _____   DO   IO   OP

Q: _____

A: _____   DO   IO   OP

3. He sent his brother a present.

Q: _____

A: _____   DO   IO   OP

Q: _____

A: _____   DO   IO   OP

40. WHAT IS AN OBJECT PRONOUN?

An **object pronoun** is a pronoun used as an object of a verb or a preposition.

IN ENGLISH

Pronouns change according to their function in the sentence. Pronouns used as subjects are studied in **What is a Subject Pronoun?**, p. 30. We use subject pronouns when we learn to conjugate verbs (see **What is a Verb Conjugation?**, p. 39). Object pronouns are used when a pronoun is either a direct object, indirect object, or object of a preposition (see **What are Objects?**, p. 132).

The form of the object pronoun is different from the form of the subject pronoun, but the same pronoun form is used as a direct object, indirect object, or an object of a preposition.

	Subject	Object
singular		
1st person	I	me
2nd person	you	you
3rd person	he	him
	she	her
	it	it
plural		
1st person	we	us
2nd person	you	you
3rd person	they	them

Here are a few examples.

> She saw *me*.
> direct object → object pronoun

> I lent *him* my car.
> indirect object → object pronoun

> They went out with *her*.
> object of a preposition → object pronoun

In English, the object pronoun is always placed after the verb or after the preposition.

IN SPANISH

As in English, the pronouns used as objects are different from the ones used as subjects. Unlike English, however, in many cases a different object pronoun is used for each kind of object: direct, indirect, and object of a preposition. You will, therefore, have to learn how to establish the function of pronouns so that you can choose the correct Spanish form.

In Spanish, the direct and indirect object pronouns are usually placed before the verb. Consult your textbook for the rules.

Spanish Direct Object Pronouns

Let us look at the Spanish direct object pronouns to see how they are selected. Since the rules for the selection of 1st and 2nd person direct object pronouns are different from the rules for the selection of 3rd person direct object pronouns, we have divided the Spanish direct object pronouns into these two categories.

1ST AND 2ND PERSON SINGULAR AND PLURAL *(me, you, us)*

The direct object pronoun of the 1st or 2nd person are merely a question of memorization. Select the form you need from the chart below and place it before the verb.

	Subject	**Direct Object**
singular		
lst person	yo	me
2nd person	tú	te
plural		
lst person	nosotros(-as)	nos
2nd person	vosotros(-as)	os

To simplify our examples, we have chosen a verb that takes a direct object in both English and Spanish, the verb *to see* (**ver**).

John sees *you.*

1. IDENTIFY THE VERB: sees (to see)
2. SELECT THE SPANISH EQUIVALENT: **ve (ver)**
3. IDENTIFY THE PRONOUN OBJECT: you
4. FUNCTION OF THE PRONOUN IN SPANISH:
   QUESTION: John sees whom? ANSWER: You.
   You is a direct object pronoun.
5. SELECT THE SPANISH EQUIVALENT: **te** or **os**

Juan **te** ve. *or* Juan **os** ve.

3RD PERSON SINGULAR AND PLURAL *(him, her, you, it, them)*

The Spanish direct object pronouns of the 3rd person have a different form depending on the gender and the number of the pronoun.

		Subject	Direct Object
singular			
masculine	*him, it*	él	lo
feminine	*her, it*	ella	la
	you	usted	lo, la
plural			
masculine	*them*	ellos	los
feminine	*them*	ellas	las
	you	ustedes	los, las

An analysis of the following sentences in which we have used each of the 3rd person English direct object pronouns will enable us to select the proper Spanish form from the chart above. We have again used the verb *to see* (**ver**) because both the English and Spanish verbs take a direct object.

"HIM"—Always masculine singular.

> *Do you see Paul? Yes, I see **him**.*
> ¿Ves a Pablo? Sí, **lo** veo.

"HER"—Always feminine singular.

> *Do you see Mary? Yes, I see **her**.*
> ¿Ves a María? Sí, **la** veo.

"YOU"—Formal singular. The gender will depend on the gender of its antecedent, i.e., the noun to which "you" refers.

> *Whom does Paul see? He sees **you**.* [when speaking to a male]
> > 1. ANTECEDENT: you
> > 2. GENDER: masculine
> > 3. SELECTION: **lo**
>
> ¿A quién ve Pablo? Pablo **lo** ve.
>
> *Whom does Paul see? He sees **you**.* [when speaking to a female]
> > 1. ANTECEDENT: you
> > 2. GENDER: feminine
> > 3. SELECTION: **la**
>
> ¿A quién ve Pablo? Pablo **la** ve.

"IT"—Always singular. The gender will depend on the gender of its antecedent, i.e., the noun "it" refers to.

*Do you see the book? Yes, I see **it**.*
  1. ANTECEDENT: **el libro** *(book)*.
  2. GENDER: masculine
  3. SELECTION: **lo**

¿Ves el libro? Sí, **lo** veo.

*Do you see the table? Yes, I see **it**.*
  1. ANTECEDENT: **la mesa** *(table)*.
  2. GENDER: feminine
  3. SELECTION: **la**

¿Ves la mesa? Sí, **la** veo.

"THEM"—Always plural. The gender will depend on the gender of its antecedent, i.e. the noun "them" refers to.

*Do you see the girls? Yes, I see **them**.*
  1. ANTECEDENT: **las chicas** *(girls)*.
  2. GENDER: feminine
  3. SELECTION: **las**

¿Ves a las chicas? Sí, **las** veo.

*Do you see the cars? Yes, I see **them**.*
  1. ANTECEDENT: **los coches** *(cars)*.
  2. GENDER: masculine
  3. SELECTION: **los**

¿Ves los coches? Sí, **los** veo.

Spanish Indirect Object Pronouns

Let us look at the Spanish indirect object pronouns to see how they are selected. Since the rules for the selection of 1st and 2nd persons indirect object pronouns are different from the rules for the selection of 3rd person indirect object pronouns, we have divided the Spanish indirect object pronouns into these two categories.

When a pronoun is used, the "to" preceding the English indirect object is not expressed in Spanish. The Spanish indirect object pronoun means "to me," "to you," etc.

1ST AND 2ND PERSON SINGULAR AND PLURAL *(me, you, us)*

The indirect object pronoun of the 1st or 2nd person are merely a question of memorization. Select the form you need from the chart below and place it before the verb.

	Subject	Indirect Object
singular		
Ist person	yo	me
2nd person	tú	te
plural		
Ist person	nosotros(-as)	nos
2nd person	vosotros(-as)	os

To simplify our examples, we have chosen a verb that takes an indirect object in both English and Spanish, the verb *to speak* (**hablar**).

> *John speaks **to me**.*
> > 1. IDENTIFY THE VERB: speaks (to speak)
> > 2. SELECT THE SPANISH EQUIVALENT: **habla (hablar)**
> > 3. IDENTIFY THE PRONOUN OBJECT: me
> > > QUESTION: John speaks to whom? ANSWER: To me.
> > > *Me* is a indirect object pronoun.
> > 4. SELECT THE SPANISH EQUIVALENT: **me**
>
> Juan **me** habla.

3RD PERSON SINGULAR AND PLURAL *(him, her, you, it, them)*

The Spanish indirect object pronouns of the 3rd person have two forms depending on the number of the pronoun.

		Subject	Indirect Object
singular			
masculine	*him, it*	él	le
feminine	*her, it*	ella	le
	you	usted	le
plural			
masculine	*them*	ellos	les
feminine	*them*	ellas	les
	you	ustedes	les

An analysis of the following sentences in which we have used each of the 3rd person English indirect object pronoun will enable us to select the proper Spanish form from the chart above. We have again used the verb *to speak* (**hablar**) because both the English and Spanish verbs take an indirect object.

"HIM, HER" OR "YOU"—Always singular.

> *To whom is John speaking? John is speaking to him.*
> 1. IDENTIFY THE VERB: is speaking (to speak)
> 2. SELECT THE SPANISH EQUIVALENT: **habla (hablar)**
> 3. IDENTIFY THE PRONOUN OBJECT: him
> 4. FUNCTION OF THE PRONOUN IN SPANISH:
>   QUESTION: John is speaking to whom? ANSWER: To him.
>   *Him* is an indirect object pronoun.
> 5. SELECT THE SPANISH EQUIVALENT: **le**

¿A quién le habla Juan? Juan **le** habla.

> *To whom is John speaking? John is speaking to her.*
> 1 - 5. See above.

¿A quién le habla Juan? Juan **le** habla.

> *To whom is John speaking? John is speaking to you.*
> 1 - 5. See above.

¿A quién le habla Juan? Juan **le** habla.

In order to distinguish **le** meaning *to him* from **le** meaning *to her* or *to you*, the phrase **a él, a ella** or **a usted** can be added to the end of the sentence.

Juan **le** habla **a él**.	*John speaks to him.*
Juan **le** habla **a ella**.	*John speaks to her.*
Juan **le** habla **a usted**.	*John speaks to you.*

"THEM"—Always plural.

> *To whom is John speaking? John is speaking to them.*
> 1. IDENTIFY THE VERB: is speaking (to speak)
> 2. SELECT THE SPANISH EQUIVALENT: **habla (hablar)**
> 3. IDENTIFY THE PRONOUN OBJECT: them
> 4. FUNCTION OF THE PRONOUN IN SPANISH:
>   QUESTION: John is speaking to whom? ANSWER: To them.
>   *Them* is an indirect object pronoun.
> 5. SELECT THE SPANISH EQUIVALENT: **les**

¿A quiénes les habla Juan? Juan **les** habla.

> *To whom is John speaking? John is speaking to you.*
> 1 - 5. See above.

¿A quiénes les habla Juan? Juan **les** habla.

In order to distinguish **les** meaning *to them* (masculine or feminine) and *to you*, the phrase **a ellos, a ellas** or **a ustedes** can be added to the end of the sentence.

Juan **les** habla **a ellos**.	*John speaks to them.* [group of males]
Juan **les** habla **a ellas**.	*John speaks to them.* [group of females]
Juan **les** habla **a ustedes**.	*John speaks to you.*

Spanish Pronouns as Objects of Prepositions

Pronouns that are objects of prepositions other than *to* have certain forms that are different from the forms used as direct or indirect objects. Unlike other object pronouns which are placed before the verb, pronouns as objects of prepositions are placed after the preposition. In this they are like nouns used as objects of prepositions.

Let us look at the Spanish object of preposition pronouns to see how they are selected. Because the rules for the selection of the object of preposition pronouns of the 1st and 2nd persons singular are different from the rules for the selection of the rest of the object of preposition pronouns, we have divided the Spanish object of preposition pronouns into three categories.

1ST AND 2ND PERSON SINGULAR (*me* and *you*)

The 1st and 2nd person singular object of preposition pronouns are merely a question of memorization. Select the form you need from the chart below and place it after the preposition.

	Subject	Object of preposition
singular		
1st person	yo	mí
2nd person	tú	ti

Is the book for John? No, it's for me.
             No, it's for you. [fam. sing.]

   1. IDENTIFY THE PREPOSITION: for
   2. IDENTIFY THE OBJECT OF THE PREPOSITION: me, you
   3. SELECTION: **mí, ti**

¿Es para Juan el libro? No, es **para mí**.
             No, es **para ti**.

1ST AND 2ND PERSON PLURAL (*us* and *you*)

The Spanish forms are different depending on the gender of the pronoun.

	Subject	Object of preposition
plural		
Ist person	nosotros(-as)	nosotros(-as)
2nd person	vosotros(-as)	vosotros(-as)

*Is the book for John? No, it's **for us**.*   [group of males]
*No, it's **for us**.*   [group of females]
*No, it's **for you**.*   [group of males]
*No, it s **for you**.*   [group of females]

   1. IDENTIFY THE PREPOSITION: for

   2. IDENTIFY THE OBJECT OF THE PREPOSITION: us, you

   3. SELECTION: **nosotros, nosotras, vosotros, vosotras**

¿Es para Juan el libro? No, es **para nosotros**.
No, es **para nosostras**.
No, es **para vosostros**.
No, es **para vosostras**.

3RD PERSON SINGULAR AND PLURAL (*him, her, you, them*)

The Spanish forms are different depending on the gender and number of the pronoun.

	Subject	Object of preposition
singular		
	él	él
	ella	ella
	usted	usted
plural		
	ellos(-as)	ellos(-as)
	ustedes	ustedes

"HIM" AND "HER"—Always singular.

*Is the book for John? Yes, it is **for him**.*

   1. IDENTIFY THE PREPOSITION: for

   2. IDENTIFY THE OBJECT OF THE PREPOSITION: him

   3. SELECTION: **él**

¿Es para Juan el libro? Sí, es **para él**.

*Is the book for Mary? Yes, it is **for her**.*
>> 1 - 5. See above.

¿Es para María el libro? Sí, es **para ella**.

"You"—Singular or plural.

*Is the book for me? Yes, it's **for you**.* [one person]
>> 1. IDENTIFY THE PREPOSITION: for
>> 2. IDENTIFY THE OBJECT OF THE PREPOSITION: me, you
>> 3. DETERMINE IF "YOU" IS SINGULAR OR PLURAL: *You* is singular.
>> 4. SELECTION: **usted**

¿Es para mí el libro? Sí, es **para usted**.

*Is the book for us? Yes, it's **for you**.* [more than one person]
>> 1 - 4. See above.

¿Es para nosotros el libro? Sí, es **para ustedes**.

In Spanish a noun referring to a thing is not generally replaced by a pronoun when it follows a preposition.

"IT"—For example, in answer to the question "Is the book on the table?" one does not say "Yes, the book is on it." Rather, one repeats the noun: "Yes, the book is on the table."

"THEM"—For example, in answer to the question "Do you live near the mountains?" one does not usually say, "Yes, I live near them." Instead, one repeats the noun or shortens the answer: "Sí, vivo cerca de las montañas" or "Sí, vivo cerca" ("Yes I live near the mountains" or "Yes, I live near").

Careful

Remember that English and Spanish verbs don't always take the same type of objects and that when working in Spanish you will have to establish the type of object taken by the Spanish verb (see p. 136-7).

Summary

Below is a flow chart of the steps you have to follow to find the Spanish equivalent of each English object pronoun. It is important that you do the steps in sequence, because each step depends on the previous one.

DO = Direct object in the Spanish sentence
IO = Indirect object in the Spanish sentence
OP = Object of a preposition in the Spanish sentence

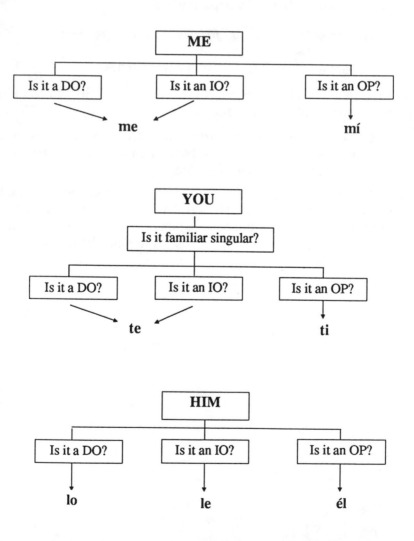

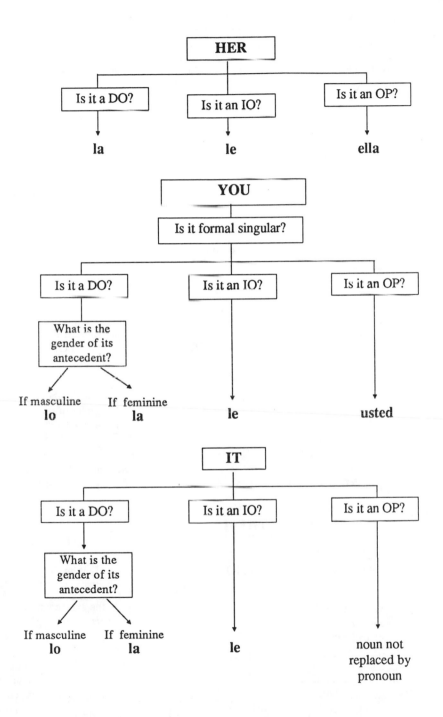

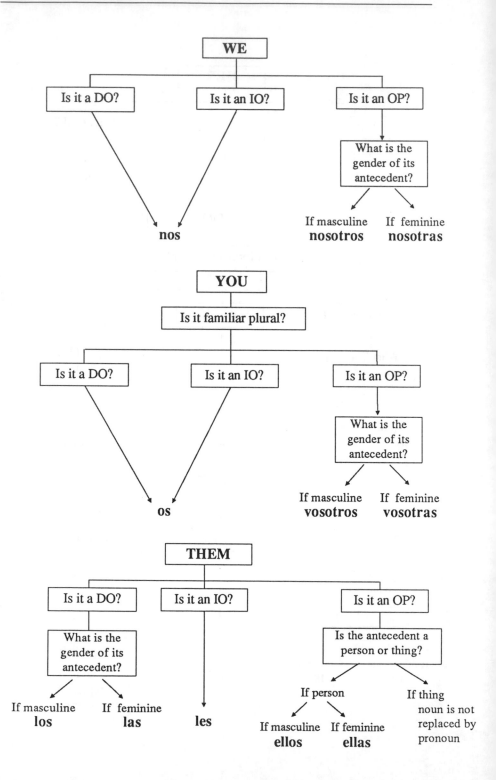

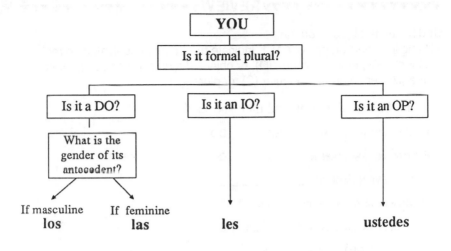

▼▼▼▼▼▼▼▼▼▼▼▼▼▼▼▼▼REVIEW▼▼▼▼▼▼▼▼▼▼▼▼▼▼▼▼▼

Underline the object pronoun.
▪ Using the chart on pp. 147-151, indicate the Spanish equivalent: direct object (DO), indirect object (IO), or object of a preposition (OP), masculine (M), feminine (F), singular (S), or plural (P).

1. Mary bought the book and then she read it.

FUNCTION OF PRONOUN IN ENGLISH: DO   IO   OP

FUNCTION OF PRONOUN IN SPANISH: DO   IO   OP

ANTECEDENT IN ENGLISH: _____

NUMBER OF ANTECEDENT IN SPANISH: S   P

GENDER OF ANTECEDENT IN SPANISH: masculine

María compró el libro y después _____ leyó.

2. Juan bought some magazines and then he read them.

FUNCTION OF PRONOUN IN ENGLISH: DO   IO   OP

FUNCTION OF PRONOUN IN SPANISH: DO   IO   OP

ANTECEDENT IN ENGLISH: _____

NUMBER OF ANTECEDENT IN SPANISH: S   P

GENDER OF ANTECEDENT IN SPANISH: feminine

Juan compró algunas revistas y después _____ leyó.

3. The teacher spoke to them about the exam yesterday.

FUNCTION OF PRONOUN IN ENGLISH: DO   IO   OP

FUNCTION OF PRONOUN IN SPANISH: DO   IO   OP

NUMBER OF PRONOUN: S   P

La profesora _____ habló del examen ayer.

4. Did you write Paul? No, but I will write him today.

FUNCTION OF PRONOUN IN ENGLISH: DO   IO   OP

FUNCTION OF PRONOUN IN SPANISH: DO   IO   OP

NUMBER OF ANTECEDENT IN SPANISH: S   P

GENDER OF ANTECEDENT IN SPANISH: M   F

¿Le escribiste a Pablo? No, pero _____ escribiré hoy.

41. WHAT IS AN INTERROGATIVE PRONOUN?

An **interrogative pronoun** is a word that replaces a noun and introduces a question. Interrogative comes from *interrogate*, to question.

IN ENGLISH
Different interrogative pronouns are used depending on whether you are referring to a "person" (this category includes human beings and live animals) or a "thing" (this category includes objects and ideas). Also, the interrogative pronoun referring to persons changes according to its function in the sentence.

IN SPANISH
As in English, a different interrogative pronoun is used depending on whether the pronoun replaces a person or a thing. The interrogative pronoun also changes according to its function in the sentence.

In English and in Spanish, an interrogative pronoun can be a subject, a direct object, an indirect object, or an object of a preposition.

"Who, Whom, Whose"

IN ENGLISH
Who is used for the subject of the sentence.

> *Who* lives here?
> subject

> *Who* are they?
> subject

Whom is used for the direct object, indirect object, and the object of a preposition.

> *Whom* do you know here?
> direct object

> To *whom* did you speak?
> indirect object

> From *whom* did you get the book?
> object of preposition *from*

In informal English, *who* is often used instead of *whom*, and prepositions are placed at the end of the sentence, separated from the interrogative pronoun to which they are linked.

Who do you know here?
|
instead of *whom*

Who did you speak to?
| |
instead of *whom*   preposition

Who did you get the book from?
| |
instead of *whom*   preposition

Whose is the possessive form and is used to ask about possession or ownership.

Whose pencil is this?
|
possessive

They are nice cars. *Whose* are they?
                              |
                         possessive

IN SPANISH
Who, *whom* and *whose* → **quién** or **quiénes.** The form used depends on the number of its antecedent, i.e., the noun the pronoun refers to.

Who—Always a subject pronoun. Since there is no English equivalent for **quiénes**, both the singular and plural forms translate alike in English.

A question with **quién** asks for a singular response.

¿**Quién** viene? Juan viene.
| |
singular subject   singular subject
Who is coming? John is coming.

A question with **quiénes** asks for a plural response.

¿**Quiénes** vienen? Juan, Roberto y Miguel vienen.
| |_____|
plural subject   plural subject
Who is coming? John, Robert and Michael are coming.

If you don't know if the response is going to be singular or plural, use the singular form.

Whom—The direct object, indirect object, and object of preposition form.

> *With **whom** are you leaving? I'm leaving with Robert.*
>   singular   singular response
> ¿Con **quién** sales? Salgo con Roberto.

> *With **whom** are you leaving? I'm leaving with my friends.*
>   plural   plural response
> ¿Con **quiénes** sales? Salgo con mis amigos.

It will often be necessary to restructure English sentences that contain *who* or *whom* separated from the preposition in order to use **quién(-es)** correctly in Spanish.

The following sentences have been restructured to avoid the dangling preposition (see p. 130).

> **Who** *are you writing **to**?*   → ***To whom** are you writing.*
> subject form of   preposition   object form of interrogative
> interrogative
> ¿**A quién** le escribes?

> **Who** *are you leaving **with**?*   → *With **whom** are you leaving?*
> subject form of   preposition   object form of interrogative
> interrogative
> ¿**Con quién** sales?

> **Who** *did you buy the gift **for**?*   → *For **whom** did you buy the gift?*
> subject form of   preposition   object form of interrogative
> interrogative
> ¿**Para quién** compraste el regalo?

Whose → **de quién(-es)**. It is the possessive interrogative. English sentences with *whose* will have to be restructured in order to use the correct word order in Spanish. To restructure replace *whose* with "of whom" and invert the word order of the subject and verb.

> *Whose car is it?*
> ¿**De quién** es el coche?
> [word-for-word: *of whom is the car*]

"What"

IN ENGLISH

What refers only to things, and the same form is used for subject, direct object, indirect object, and the object of a preposition.

> *What* happened?
> |
> subject

> *What* do you want?
> |
> direct object

> *What* do you cook with?
> |
> object of preposition *with*

IN SPANISH

What → **qué** has only one form since it is invariable.[1]

> ***What*** *are you studying this semester?*
> ¿**Qué** estudias este semestre?

> ***What*** *is that?*
> ¿**Qué** es esto?

"Which one, Which ones"

IN ENGLISH

Which one, *which ones* can refer to both persons and things; they are used in questions that request the selection of one (*which one*, singular) or several (*which ones*, plural) from a group. The words *one* and *ones* are often omitted. These interrogative pronouns may be used as a subject, direct object, indirect object, and object of a preposition.

> All the teachers are here. *Which one* teaches Spanish?
> |
> singular subject

> I have two cars. *Which one* do you want to take?
> |
> singular direct object

---

[1]**Qué** can also be used as an interrogative adjective (see p. 113). As an interrogative adjective **qué** is followed by a noun and means *what* or *which:* ¿**Qué** libro tienes? ***Which*** *book do you have?*

There are many children here. With *which ones* do you want to speak?

plural object of the preposition *with*

IN SPANISH

Which one or *which ones* → **cuál** or **cuáles**. There are two forms to agree in number with the noun replaced, *which one* (singular) or *which ones* (plural).

Which one do you need?
¿**Cuál** necesitas?

Which ones do you need?
¿**Cuáles** necesitas?

If the English word *one* or *ones* is not expressed, look at the verb, if it is singular, use **cuál**; if the verb is plural, use **cuáles**.

Which of the girls is Spanish?
¿**Cuál** de las chicas **es** española?

Which of the girls are Spanish?
¿**Cuáles** de las chicas **son** españolas?

Careful

Which is or *which are* → **qué** + **ser** or **cuál(-es)** + **ser**. To determine which to use you need to decide what the expected answer will be.

- **qué** + **ser** is used when the expected answer is a definition

  What is the Nobel Prize?
      The expected answer is a definition of the Nobel Prize.
  ¿**Qué es** el Premio Nobel?

  What are the Panamerican Games?
      The expected answer is a definition of the Panamerican Games.
  ¿**Qué son** los Juegos Panamericanos?

- **cuál (-es)** + **ser** is used when the expected answer provides one of a number of choices and answers the question *which one(-s)* of many. If the "what" of the English question means *which one* or *which ones*, then use **cuál(-es)**.

  What is your favorite novel?
      The expected answer will explain which novel of the many that exist is the favorite.
  ¿**Cuál es** su novela favorita?

What are the countries of Europe?

> The expected answer will explain which countries of the many in the world are European.

¿**Cuáles son** los países de Europa?

There is another interrogative pronoun that we will now examine separately since it does not follow the same pattern as above.

"How much, How many" → cuánto(-a), cuántos(-as)

IN ENGLISH

These interrogative pronouns are a rare example of pronouns that change form to agree in number with the noun they replace.

How much money do you need?
   singular pronoun

How many stamps do you need?
   plural pronoun

IN SPANISH

This interrogative pronoun has four forms that change according to the gender and number of the antecedent, that is, the noun replaced by the pronoun.

	Singular	Plural
masculine	cuánto	cuántos
feminine	cuánta	cuántas

Let us look at a few examples.

*I have a lot of paper. **How much** do you want?*
   1. IDENTIFY ANTECEDENT: **el papel** *(paper)*
   2. GENDER OF ANTECEDENT: masculine
   3. NUMBER OF ANTECEDENT: singular
   4. SELECTION: **cuánto**

Tengo mucho papel. ¿**Cuánto** quieres?

*I have a lot of soup. **How much** do you want?*
   1. IDENTIFY ANTECEDENT: **la sopa** *(soup)*
   2. GENDER OF ANTECEDENT: feminine
   3. NUMBER OF ANTECEDENT: singular
   4. SELECTION: **cuánta**

Tengo mucha sopa. ¿**Cuánta** quieres?

*I have a lot of books. **How many** do you want?*
　　1. ANTECEDENT: **los libros** *(books)*
　　2. GENDER: masculine
　　3. NUMBER: plural
　　4. SELECTION: **cuántos**

Tengo muchos libros. ¿**Cuántos** quieres?

*I have a lot of magazines. **How many** do you want?*
　　1. ANTECEDENT: **las revistas** *(magazines)*
　　2. GENDER: feminine
　　3. NUMBER: plural
　　4. SELECTION: **cuántas**

Tengo muchas revistas. ¿**Cuántas** quieres?

▼▼▼▼▼▼▼▼▼▼▼▼▼▼▼▼▼REVIEW▼▼▼▼▼▼▼▼▼▼▼▼▼▼▼▼▼

Underline the interrogative pronouns in the questions below.
- Indicate the function of the interrogative pronoun in the Spanish sentence: subject (S), object (O), or possessive (P).
- Fill in the Spanish equivalent of the interrogative.

1. Whose sweater is this?

　　FUNCTION:　　　S　　O　　P

　　RESTRUCTURE THE SENTENCE: _____

　　¿ _____ es este suéter?

2. Who are you talking to?

　　FUNCTION:　　　S　　O　　P

　　RESTRUCTURE THE SENTENCE: _____

　　¿A _____ le hablas?

3. Who is coming to see you? My friends.

　　FUNCTION:　　　S　　O　　P

　　¿ _____ vienen a verte? Mis amigos.

42. WHAT IS A DEMONSTRATIVE PRONOUN?

A **demonstrative pronoun** is a word that replaces a noun previously mentioned, the antecedent, as if pointing to it. Demonstrative comes from *demonstrate,* to show.

IN ENGLISH

English demonstrative pronouns change form according to the number of the noun they replace and according to the relationship of that noun with the speaker.

As with the demonstrative adjectives, *this (one)*, *these* refer to a person or an object near the speaker; *that (one)*, *those* to a person or an object away from the speaker.

> Here are two suitcases. *This one* is big and *that one* is small.
> The books are on the shelves. *These* are in Spanish, *those* in English.

IN SPANISH

Demonstrative pronouns are the same words as the demonstrative adjectives, except that all pronoun forms carry a written accent mark in order to distinguish the pronouns from the adjectives (see **What is a Demonstrative Adjective?**, p. 116).

To POINT OUT ▼	SINGULAR		PLURAL	
	masculine	feminine	masculine	feminine
items near the speaker	éste	ésta	éstos	éstas
items near the the person spoken to	ése	ésa	ésos	ésas
items away from the speaker and person spoken to	aquél	aquélla	aquéllos	aquéllas

As pronouns, these words replace the demonstrative adjective + noun; they will agree in number and gender with the noun replaced.

To choose the correct form, follow these steps.

1. Determine the antecedent.
2. Determine the gender and number of the antecedent.
3. Determine the relationship of the antecedent to the speaker or person spoken to.
4. Based on Steps 1 and 2 choose the correct form from the chart.

Let us apply these steps to some examples.

*Give me the magazine; **this one**.*

1. ANTECEDENT: **la revista** *(magazine)*
2. GENDER AND NUMBER: feminine singular
3. RELATIONSHIP: near the speaker
4. SELECTION: **ésta**

Déme la revista; **ésta**.

*Give me the books; **these (ones)**.*

1. ANTECEDENT: **los libros** *(books)*
2. GENDER AND NUMBER: masculine plural
3. RELATIONSHIP: near the speaker
4. SELECTION: **éstos**

Déme los libros; **éstos**.

*Give me the pencil near you; **that one**.*

1. ANTECEDENT: **el lápiz** *(pencil)*
2. GENDER AND NUMBER: masculine singular
3. RELATIONSHIP: near the person spoken to
4. SELECTION: **ése**

Déme el lápiz; **ése**.

*Give me the notebooks over there; **those (ones)**.*

1. ANTECEDENT: **los cuadernos** *(notebooks)*
2. GENDER AND NUMBER: masculine plural
3. RELATIONSHIP: away from the speaker and person spoken to
4. SELECTION: **aquéllos**

Déme los cuadernos; **aquéllos**.

Neuter Demonstrative Pronouns

Spanish also has three demonstrative pronouns that are used to refer to an idea, item, or previous statement which has no gender or whose gender is not known. These pronouns are therefore said to be neuter in gender and are invariable, that is, they do not change form.

esto	*this (one)*
eso	*that (one)*
aquello	*that (one)*

*What is **this**?*

Since it isn't known what "this" is, its gender is also unknown.

¿Qué es **esto**?

***That**'s not true.*

> *That* refers to a previous statement which has no gender.

Eso no es verdad.

*What is **that** over there?*

> Since it isn't known what "that" is, its gender is also unknown.

¿Qué es **aquello**?

There is another demonstrative pronoun which we will now examine separately because it does not follow the same pattern as above.

"The one, The ones"

IN ENGLISH

The demonstrative pronouns ***the one*** and ***the ones***, unlike *this one* and *that one*, do not point out a specific object, but instead introduce a clause that gives us additional information about the object and helps us identify it. There is a singular form *the one* and a plural form *the ones*. They are often followed by the relative pronoun *that* or *which* (see **What is a Relative Pronoun?**, p. 169).

> What book are you reading?
> I am reading *the one (that)* I bought yesterday.
> > CLAUSE: "the one that I bought yesterday " gives us additional information about the book. Notice that the relative pronoun "that" can be omitted in English.
> > NUMBER: *The on*e is singular.

> Which houses do you prefer?
> I prefer *the ones that* are on Columbus Street.
> > CLAUSE: "the ones that are on Columbus Street" gives us additional information about the houses.
> > NUMBER: *The ones* is plural.

IN SPANISH

Forms of the definite article **el, la, los, las** are used as the equivalent of the English demonstrative *the one(s)*. The definite article agrees in number and gender with the noun replaced. *The one* or *the ones* can be used 1. to introduce a clause and 2. to show possession.

1. to introduce a clause → the definite article + **que**

The relative pronoun *that* or **que** in Spanish (see **What is a Relative Pronoun?**, p. 169) is often omitted in English. However, the relative pronoun *that* must be expressed in Spanish.

To choose the correct form of *the one(s)* follow these steps.

1. Find the antecedent.
2. Determine the gender and number of the antecedent.
3. Select the proper form of the definite article + **que**.

Let us apply these steps to some examples.

*What book are you reading? **The one (that)** I bought yesterday.*

1. ANTECEDENT: **el libro** *(book)*
2. GENDER AND NUMBER OF ANTECEDENT: masculine singular
3. SELECTION: **el que**

¿Qué libro lees? **El que** compré ayer.

*Which houses do you prefer? **The ones (that)** are on Columbus St.*

1. ANTECEDENT: **las casas** *(houses)*
2. GENDER AND NUMBER OF ANTECEDENT: feminine plural
3. SELECTION: **las que**

¿Qué casas prefieres? **Las que** están en la calle Colón.

2. to show possession → the definite article + **de**

Whose house are you living in? My *father's*.

Just as "my father's house" can only be expressed in Spanish by the structure "the house of my father," a similar Spanish structure must be used to say "my father's." In this case the word-for-word English translation of the Spanish structure is "the one of my father." In Spanish "the one" agrees in gender and number with its antecedent, here "the house."

To choose the correct form, follow these steps.

1. Restructure the possessive phrase.
2. Find the antecedent of *the one* or *the ones*.
3. Determine the gender and number of the antecedent.
4. Select the proper form of the definite article + **de**.

Let us apply the rules to the following examples.

Which house are you selling? My father's.

1. RESTRUCTURE: My father's → the one of my father
2. ANTECEDENT: house (**la casa**)
3. GENDER AND NUMBER OF ANTECEDENT: **la casa** is feminine singular.
4. SELECTION: **la de**

¿Qué casa vendes? **La de** mi padre.

Which books are you reading? The teacher's.
>   1. RESTRUCTURE: The teacher's → the ones of the teacher
>   2. ANTECEDENT: books (**los libros**)
>   3. GENDER AND NUMBER OF ANTECEDENT: **los libros** is masculine plural.
>   4. SELECTION: **los de**

¿Qué libros lees? **Los del** profesor.

▼▼▼▼▼▼▼▼▼▼▼▼▼▼▼▼▼REVIEW▼▼▼▼▼▼▼▼▼▼▼▼▼▼▼▼▼

Circle the demonstrative pronouns in the following sentences.
- Draw an arrow from the demonstrative pronoun to its antecedent.
- Indicate if the antecedent is singular (S) or plural (P).
- Indicate the relationship: near the speaker (NS), near the person spoken to (NPS), or away from both (A).
- Fill in the Spanish demonstrative pronoun in the Spanish sentences.

1. She did not buy my house because she wants this one.

   ANTECEDENT IN SPANISH: feminine   S   P

   RELATIONSHIP TO SPEAKER: NS   NPS   A

   Ella no compró mi casa porque quiere _____.

2. Which notebook is yours? That one?

   ANTECEDENT IN SPANISH: masculine   S   P

   RELATIONSHIP TO SPEAKER: NS   NPS   A

   ¿Qué cuaderno es tuyo? ¿_____?

3. The new houses are more expensive than those over there.

   ANTECEDENT IN SPANISH: feminine   S   P

   RELATIONSHIP TO SPEAKER: NS   NPS   A

   Las casas nuevas son más caras que _____.

43. WHAT IS A POSSESSIVE PRONOUN?

A **possessive pronoun** is a word that replaces a noun and indicates the possessor of that noun. Possessive comes from *possess,* to own.

> Whose house is that? It's *mine.*

Mine is a pronoun that replaces the words "my house" and shows who possesses the house.

IN ENGLISH
Here is a list of the possessive pronouns.

Singular

1st person	mine
2nd person	yours
3rd person	⎰ his ⎱ hers ⎰ its

Plural

1st person	ours
2nd person	yours
3rd person	theirs

Possessive pronouns never change their form, regardless of the thing possessed; they refer primarily to the possessor.

> Is that your house? Yes, it's *mine.*
> Are those your keys? Yes, they're *mine.*

The same possessive pronoun *(mine)* is used, although the objects possessed are different in number *(house* is singular, *keys* is plural).

> John's car is blue. *His* is blue.
> Mary's car is blue. *Hers* is blue.

Although the object possessed is the same *(car),* the possessive pronoun is different because the possessor is different *(John* is masculine singular; *Mary* is feminine singular).

IN SPANISH
The possessive pronouns have the same forms as the stressed possessive adjectives (see p. 109 in **What is a Possessive Adjective?**). Like English, a Spanish possessive pronoun refers to the possessor, but unlike English, it must agree, like all Spanish pronouns, in gender and number with its antecedent. Therefore, there are masculine and feminine forms in both the singular and plural.

In the example below, in the phrase **los míos** *(mine)*, the first letters of the possessive pronoun **mí-** refer to the 1st person singular possessor *(mine)* and the ending of the possessive pronoun **(-os)** and the definite article agree with the noun possessed **libros** *(books)* which is masculine plural.

The first letters of the possessive pronoun refer to the possessor and the ending of the possessive pronoun agrees with the noun possessed.

> *Where are your books? **Mine** are in the living room.*
>
> masc. pl. endings
> ¿Dónde están tus libros? **Los míos** están en la sala.
>
> 1st pers. sing. possessor

Here are the steps you should follow in choosing the correct possessive pronoun.

1. Indicate the possessor. This is shown by the first letters of the possessive pronoun.

mine	mí-
yours	tuy-
his, hers, yours	suy-
ours	nuestr-
yours	vuestr-
theirs, yours	suy-

2. Find the noun possessed and determine its gender and number. Choose the definite article + the possessive pronoun ending according to the gender and number of that noun.

   - if the noun possessed is masculine singular → use the definite article **el** and add **-o** to the first letters of the possessor.

     > *Where is the book? **Mine** is on the table.*
     >
     > noun possessed
     > masc. sing.

     ¿Dónde está el libro? **El mío** está sobre la mesa.

   - if the noun possessed is feminine singular → use the definite article **la** and add **-a** to the first letters of the possessor.

     > *Where is the magazine? **Mine** is on the table.*
     >
     > noun possessed
     > fem. sing.

     ¿Dónde está la revista? **La mía** está sobre la mesa.

- if the noun possessed is masculine plural→ use the definite article **los** and add **-os** to the first letters of the possessor.

> *Where are the books? **Mine** are on the table.*
> |
> noun possessed
> masc. pl.

¿Dónde están los libros? **Los míos** están sobre la mesa.

- if the noun possessed is feminine plural→ use the definite article **las** and add **-as** to the first letters of the possessor.

> *Where are the magazines? **Mine** are on the table.*
> |
> noun possessed
> fem. pl.

¿Dónde están las revistas? **Las mías** están sobre la mesa.

3. Select the proper form.

Let us apply the steps to the following examples.

> *She is reading her magazines. He is reading **yours**.*
> 1. INDICATE THE POSSESSOR: **tuy-**
> 2. INDICATE THE NOUN POSSESSED AND ITS NUMBER AND GENDER:
>   *Magazines* (**las revistas**) is feminine plural.
> 3. SELECTION: **las + -as**

Ella lee sus revistas. El lee **las tuyas**.

> *Susana forgot her notebook but we have **ours**.*
> 1. INDICATE THE POSSESSOR: **nuestr-**
> 2. INDICATE THE NOUN POSSESSED AND ITS NUMBER AND GENDER:
>   *Notebook* (**el cuaderno**) is masculine singular.
> 3. SELECTION: **el + -o**

Susana olvidó su cuaderno pero tenemos **el nuestro**.

Careful

The definite article is not used when the possessive pronoun follows a form of the verb **ser** *(to be)*.

> *Is this your coat? No, it's not **mine**. **Mine** is larger.*
> ¿Es éste tu abrigo? No, no es **mío**. **El mío** es más grande.
> | ⌐————
> possessive pronoun   article + possessive
> without article   pronoun
> after **ser**

▼▼▼▼▼▼▼▼▼▼▼▼▼▼▼▼▼▼▼REVIEW▼▼▼▼▼▼▼▼▼▼▼▼▼▼▼▼▼▼▼

Underline the possessive pronouns in the sentences below.
- Draw an arrow from the possessive pronoun to its antecedent.
- Indicate whether the antecedent is singular (S) or plural (P).
- Fill in the Spanish possessive pronoun in the Spanish sentences.

1. I won't take your car. I'll take mine.

   ANTECEDENT IN SPANISH: masculine   S   P

   No tomaré tu coche. Tomaré _____

2. I'm not going with my parents. I'm going with hers.

   ANTECEDENT IN SPANISH: masculine   S   P

   No voy con mis padres. Voy con _____

3. These aren't your (fam. sing.) boots. Yours are bigger.

   ANTECEDENT IN SPANISH: feminine   S   P

   No son tus botas. _____ son más grandes.

4. Paul's racquet is broken; he'll use ours.

   ANTECEDENT IN SPANISH: feminine   S   P

   La raqueta de Pablo está rota. Va a usar _____

44. WHAT IS A RELATIVE PRONOUN?

A **relative pronoun** is a word that serves two purposes:

1. As a pronoun it stands for a noun or another pronoun previously mentioned. The noun or pronoun referred to is called **the antecedent**.

> This is the boy *who* broke the window.
> |
>   antecedent

2. It introduces a **subordinate clause,** that is, a group of words having a subject and verb separate from the subject and verb of the main sentence. A subordinate clause does not express a complete thought. A main clause can stand alone as a complete sentence.

>   main clause   subordinate clause
> ┌   ┐ ┌   ┐
> This is the boy *who* broke the window.
> | |
>   subject verb

> ["who broke the window" is not a complete sentence]

The above subordinate clause is also called a **relative clause** because it starts with the relative pronoun *who*. The relative clause gives us additional information about the antecedent *boy*.

Relative clauses are very common. We use them in our everyday speech without giving much thought to why and how we construct them. The relative pronoun allows us to combine in a single sentence two thoughts which have a common element.

> **sentence a**   I met *the teacher.*
> **sentence b**   *He* teaches Spanish in my school.
> **combined**   I met *the teacher who* teaches Spanish in my school.

When sentences are combined with a relative pronoun, the relative pronoun can have different functions in the relative clause. It can be the subject, the direct object, the indirect object, or the object of a preposition. Since your selection of the relative pronoun will depend on its function, we shall study each function separately.

IN ENGLISH

In an English sentence, the relative pronoun is often omitted.

> The book I'm reading is interesting.
> The book *that* I'm reading is interesting.
> |
>   relative pronoun

In many cases the selection of a relative pronoun depends not only on its function in the relative clause, but also on whether the antecedent is a "person" (this category includes human beings and live animals) or a "thing" (this category includes objects and ideas).

IN SPANISH

Relative pronouns are used just as they are in English. The main difference is that, unlike English, where the relative pronoun can sometimes be omitted at the beginning of a relative clause, the relative pronoun must always be expressed.[1]

Subject of the Relative Clause

IN ENGLISH

There are three relative pronouns that can be used as subjects of a relative clause, depending on whether the relative pronoun refers to a person or to a thing.

"Person"

Who or *that* is used for the subject of the sentence.

> She is the only student *who* answered all the time.
> |
> antecedent
>
> *Who* is the subject of *answered.*

> She is the only student *that* answered all the time.
> |
> antecedent
>
> *That* is the subject of *answered.*

"Thing"

Which or *that* is used for the subject of the sentence.

> The movie *which* is so popular was filmed in Spain.
> |
> antecedent
> *Which* is the subject of *is.*

> The movie *that* is so popular was filmed in Spain.
> |
> antecedent
> *That* is the subject of *is.*

---

[1]This handbook will deal with the relative pronouns **que**, **quien(-es)**, and **lo que**. Forms of **el que**, **el cual**, and the relative adjective **cuyo** are not included since most beginning textbooks do not treat them.

IN SPANISH

Que is used as the subject of a relative clause, regardless of whether the antecedent is a person or a thing. **Que** is invariable.

> *John is the student **that (who)** answered.*
> |
>   antecedent person
> *That (who)* is the subject of *answered.*

Juan es el estudiante **que** respondió.

> *This is the phone **that (which)** isn't working.*
> |
>   antecedent thing
> *That (which)* is the subject of *isn't working.*

Aquí está el teléfono **que** no funciona.

Combining Sentences With a Relative Pronoun Subject

IN ENGLISH

> **sentence a**   The students passed the exam.
> **sentence b**   They studied.

1. Identify the element the two sentences have in common.

   The students and *they;* both words refer to the same persons.

2. The relative pronoun always replaces the element which the second sentence has in common with the first sentence.

   They will be replaced by a relative pronoun.

3. The relative pronoun in the relative clause will have the same function as the word it replaces.

   They is the subject of *studied.* The relative pronoun will be the subject of *studied.*

4. Choose the relative pronoun according to whether its antecedent is a person or a thing.

   They refers to *students.* Therefore, its antecedent is a person.

5. Select the relative pronoun.

   Who or *that* is the subject relative pronoun referring to a person.

6. Place the relative pronoun right after its antecedent.

   > The students *who* studied passed the exam.
   > The students *that* studied passed the exam.
   > | |_____|
   > antecedent   relative clause

IN SPANISH

sentence a	Los estudiantes aprobaron el examen.
sentence b	Estudiaron.

Follow the same steps as under In English above, skipping step 4.

Los estudiantes **que** estudiaron aprobaron el examen.
| antecedent | relative clause |

Direct Object of the Relative Clause

IN ENGLISH

There are three relative pronouns that can be used as direct objects of a relative clause, depending on whether the relative pronoun refers to a person or a thing. We have indicated relative pronouns in parentheses because they are often omitted.

"Person"
Whom or *that* is used as a direct object of a sentence.

This is the student *(whom)* I saw yesterday.
        antecedent
Whom is the direct object of *saw.*
(I is the subject of the relative clause.)

This is the student *(that)* I saw yesterday.
        antecedent
That is the direct object of *saw.*
(I is the subject of the relative clause.)

"Thing"
Which or *that* is used as a direct object of a sentence.

This is the book *(which)* Paul bought.
        antecedent
Which is the direct object of *bought.*
(Paul is the subject of the relative clause.)

This is the book *(that)* Paul bought.
        antecedent
That is the direct object of *bought.*
(Paul is the subject of the relative clause.)

IN SPANISH
Que is used as the direct object of a relative clause, regardless of whether the antecedent is a person or a thing. **Que** is invariable.

We have included the relative pronouns in the English sentences below to show you what the Spanish relative pronoun relates to; however, since the relative pronoun is often omitted in an English sentence, we have put them between parentheses.

> *This is the student (**that** or **whom**) John saw last night.*
> |
>   antecedent person
> *That* or *whom* is the direct object of *saw.*
> *(Juan* is the subject of the relative clause.)

Este es el estudiante **que** Juan vio anoche.

> *This is the book (**which** or **that**) John bought.*
> |
>   antecedent thing
> *Which* or *that* is the direct object of *bought.*
> *(John* is the subject of the relative clause.)

Este es el libro **que** Juan compró.

Combining Sentences with a Relative Pronoun Direct Object

IN ENGLISH

> **sentence a**   The Spanish teacher is nice.
> **sentence b**   I met her today.

> 1. COMMON ELEMENT: *the Spanish teacher* and *her*
> 2. ELEMENT TO BE REPLACED: her
> 3. FUNCTION OF *HER:* direct object
> 4. ANTECEDENT: *the Spanish teacher* is a person
> 5. SELECTION: *whom* or *that*
> 6. PLACEMENT: *whom* or *that* after *the Spanish teacher*

The Spanish teacher *(whom)* I met today is nice.
The Spanish teacher I met today is nice.

Notice that the relative pronoun *whom* is left out in spoken English, making it difficult to identify the two clauses.

IN SPANISH

> **sentence a**   La profesora de español es simpática.
> **sentence b**   La conocí hoy.

Follow the same steps as under In English above, skipping step 4.

> La profesora de español **que** conocí hoy es simpática.
> |_____| |_____|
>   antecedent   relative clause

Indirect Object or Object of Preposition in the Relative Clause

Both the relative pronoun as an indirect object and the relative pronoun as an object of a preposition involve prepositions.

It is difficult to identify the function of a relative pronoun because in English a preposition is often placed at the end of the sentence, separated from the relative pronoun to which it is linked. This separation of a preposition from its object is called a **dangling preposition** (see p. 130).

To make it easier for you to identify a relative pronoun as an indirect object or as an object of a preposition, you will have to change the structure of the sentence so that the preposition is placed before the pronoun. This restructuring will not only make it easier for you to identify the function of the pronoun, but will also establish the word order for the Spanish sentence.

IN ENGLISH
There are two relative pronouns used as indirect objects, depending on whether you are referring to a person or a thing.

"Person"
Whom is used as an indirect object or as an object of a preposition.

> Here is the student I was speaking to.
> |
>   antecedent

This English structure cannot be translated word-for-word into Spanish for two reasons:

1. The Spanish language does not permit dangling prepositions, and

2. the relative pronoun omitted in English must be expressed in Spanish. To establish the Spanish structure, you must restructure the English sentence, placing the preposition within the sentence and adding a relative pronoun. If you are not sure where to place the preposition and the relative pronoun, remember that they follow immediately after the antecedent.

> | Spoken English | → | Restructured |
> |---|---|---|
> | Here is the student | | Here is the student *to* |
> | I was speaking *to*. | | *whom* I was speaking. |

> *Whom* is the indirect object of *was speaking*.

> Here is the student I was talking about.
> |
>   antecedent

As in the case of the indirect object, spoken English often omits the relative pronoun and places the preposition at the end of the sentence.

Spoken English	→	**Restructured**
Here is the student I was speaking *about.*		Here is the student *about whom* I was speaking.

Whom is the object of the preposition *about.*

Here is the student *about whom* I was speaking.
          antecedent   relative clause

"Thing"
Which is used as an indirect object or as an object of a preposition.

Here is the museum he gave a painting to.
          antecedent

Spoken English	→	**Restructured**
Here is the museum he gave the painting *to.*		Here is the museum *to which* he gave the painting.

Which is the indirect object of *gave.*

Here is the museum *to which* he gave the painting.
          antecedent   relative clause

IN SPANISH

"Person"
Quien or **quienes** is used as the indirect object as well as the object of a preposition of a relative clause. You will often need to restructure the English sentence before attempting to put it into Spanish.

John is the boy I'm going with.   **Restructured** →
   singular antecedent   preposition
*John is the boy **with whom** I am going.*
         preposition object of preposition
Juan es el chico **con quien** salgo.

The girls I'm writing to live in Madrid.   **Restructured** →
 plural antecedent   preposition
*The girls **to whom** I am writing live in Madrid.*
      preposition object of preposition
Las chicas **a quienes** les escribo viven en Madrid.

"Thing"

In conversational Spanish a preposition + **que** is generally used.

> *This is the book I was talking about.*   **Restructured →**
> | |
>   antecedent   preposition
>
> *This is the book **about which** I was talking.*
> | |
>   preposition   object of preposition

Este es el libro **de que** hablaba.

The following chart provides a summary of the relative pronouns.

ENGLISH		SPANISH	
subject		**subject**	
person	*who, that*	person	**que**
thing	*that, which*	thing	**que**
direct object		**direct object**	
person	*whom, that*	person	**que**
thing	*that, which*	thing	**que**
object of preposition		**object of preposition**	
person	*whom*	person	preposition + **quien(-es)**
thing	*which*	thing	preposition + **que**

To find the correct relative pronoun you must go through the following steps.

1. **RELATIVE CLAUSE**—Find the relative clause. Restructure the English clause if there is a dangling preposition and add the relative pronoun if it has been omitted.

2. **FUNCTION OF PRONOUN**—Establish the function of the relative pronoun in the Spanish sentence.

   SUBJECT—if the relative pronoun is the subject of the English sentence, it will be the subject of the Spanish sentence → **que**

   DIRECT OBJECT—if the Spanish verb takes a direct object → **quien**

   INDIRECT OBJECT OR OBJECT OF A PREPOSITION—if a PERSON → preposition + **quien (-es)**, if a THING → preposition + **que**

3. **SELECTION**—Select the Spanish form.

Let us apply these steps to some examples.

*The lady **who** is my neighbor is from Colombia.*
>   1. RELATIVE CLAUSE: who is my neighbor
>   2. FUNCTION RELATIVE PRONOUN IN SPANISH: subject of the relative clause
>   3. SELECTION: **que**

La señora **que** es mi vecina es de Ecuador.

Peter and Joe are the boys I was talking to.

Spoken English	→	Restructured
Peter and Joe are the boys I was talking *to*.		Peter and Joe are the boys *to whom* I was talking.

>   1. RELATIVE CLAUSE: I was talking to → to whom I was talking
>   2. FUNCTION RELATIVE PRONOUN IN SPANISH: object of preposition *to*
>   3. SELECTION: **quienes**

Pedro y José son los chicos **a quienes** hablaba.

Relative pronouns can be tricky to handle and this handbook provides only a simple outline. Refer to your Spanish textbook for additional rules.

Relative Pronouns Without Antecedent

There are relative pronouns that do not refer to a specific noun or pronoun within the same sentence. Instead these relative pronouns refer back to a whole idea or to an antecedent that is not expressed.

IN ENGLISH

There are two relative pronouns that may be used without an antecedent: *what* and *which*.

What—not referring to any specific noun or pronoun.[1]

> I don't know *what* happened.
> |
> no expressed antecedent
> subject

> Here is *what* I read.
> |
> no expressed antecedent
> direct object

---

[1]The relative pronoun *what* (meaning *that which*) should not be confused with other uses of *what:* as an interrogative pronoun (***What** do you want?* ¿**Qué** quieres?, see p. 153), and as an interrogative adjective (***What** book do you want?* ¿**Qué** libro quieres?, see p. 113).

Which—referring back to an idea, not to a specific noun or pronoun.

You speak many languages, *which* is an asset.

> antecedent → the fact that you speak many languages

She didn't do well, *which* is too bad.

> antecedent → the fact that she didn't do well

IN SPANISH

Lo que is the equivalent of the English *what* or *which* without antecedent. It is used in conversational Spanish and refers to an idea or previously mentioned statement or concept which has no gender. It can function as a subject or object.

Let us apply these rules to the following examples.

What bothers me most is the heat.

1. RELATIVE PRONOUN: what bothers me most
2. ANTECEDENT: none expressed in the sentence
3. FUNCTION RELATIVE PRONOUN IN SPANISH: subject of relative clause
4. SELECTION: **lo que**

Lo que me molesta más es el calor.

What you are saying isn't true.

1. RELATIVE PRONOUN: what you are saying
2. ANTECEDENT: none expressed in the sentence
3. FUNCTION RELATIVE PRONOUN IN SPANISH: direct object of **decir** *(to say)*
4. SELECTION: **lo que**

Lo que dices no es verdad.

*He doesn't speak Spanish, **which** will be a problem.*

1. RELATIVE PRONOUN: which will be a problem
2. ANTECEDENT: entire previous relative clause
3. FUNCTION RELATIVE PRONOUN IN SPANISH: subject of relative clause
4. SELECTION: **lo que**

No habla español **lo que** será un problema.

▼▼▼▼▼▼▼▼▼▼▼▼▼▼▼▼REVIEW▼▼▼▼▼▼▼▼▼▼▼▼▼▼▼▼

Underline the relative pronoun in the sentences below.
- Draw an arrow to the antecedent.
- Indicate the function of the relative pronoun: subject (S), direct object (DO), indirect object (IO), object of a preposition (OP), or possessive (P).
- Fill in the Spanish relative pronoun in the Spanish sentences below.

1. I received the letter that you sent me.

   FUNCTION IN SPANISH: S   DO   IO   OP   P

   Recibí la carta _____ me envió.

2. That is the woman who speaks Spanish.

   FUNCTION IN SPANISH: S   DO   IO   OP   P

   Esa es la mujer _____ habla español.

3. Paul is the student I traveled with.

   RESTRUCTURE THE SENTENCE: _____

   FUNCTION IN SPANISH: S   DO   IO   OP   P

   Pablo es el estudiante con _____ viajé.

4. What he said was a lie.

   FUNCTION IN SPANISH: S   DO   IO   OP   P

   _____ dijo fue una mentira.

45. WHAT ARE INDEFINITES AND NEGATIVES?

Indefinites are words that refer to persons, things, or periods of time that are not specific or that are not clearly defined.

IN ENGLISH

Some common indefinites are *someone, anybody, something, some day*. These indefinite words are often paired with negative words which are opposite in meaning: *no one, nobody, nothing*, and *never*.

Indefinites	Negatives
someone anyone }	no one
somebody anybody }	no body
something anything }	nothing
some day any day }	never

In conversation indefinites frequently appear in questions while negatives appear in answers.

question	Is *anyone* coming tonight?
answer	*No one.*
question	Do you have *anything* for me?
answer	*Nothing.*
question	Are you going to Europe *some day*?
answer	*Never.*

English sentences can be made negative in one of two ways (see **What are Affirmative and Negative Sentences?**, p. 47).

- the word *not* appears before the main verb

    I am studying.
    I am *not* studying.

- a negative word can be used in any part of the sentence

    No one is coming.
    He has *never* seen a movie.

English allows only one negative word (either *not* or any of the other negative words) in a sentence (or clause). When a sentence contains the word *not*, another negative word cannot be used in that sentence.

"I am not studying *nothing*." [incorrect English]
|
negative word
This sentence contains a double negative: *not* and *nothing*.

When a sentence contains the word *not*, the indefinite word that is the opposite of the negative word must be used.

I am not studying *anything*.
|
indefinite word

Let us look at another example.

I have *nothing*.
|
negative word
Nothing is the one negative word.

I do *not* have *anything*.
|
indefinite word
This sentence contains *not*; therefore, the word *anything* is substituted for *nothing*.

"I do *not* have *nothing*." [incorrect English]

This sentence contains a double negative: *not* and *nothing*.

IN SPANISH

As in English, the indefinite and negative words exist as pairs of opposites. Here is a chart of the most common indefinites and negatives.

Indefinites		Negatives	
something	algo	nada	*nothing*
some, any	{ algún / alguno	ningún / ninguno }	*none*
someone *somebody*	alguien	nadie	*no one* *nobody*
some day *always* *sometimes*	algún día siempre a veces	nunca	*never*
also, too	también	tampoco	*not...either*
either, or	o	ni	*neither...nor*

Notice that most indefinites begin with the letters **alg-** and the negatives begin with **n-**.

Contrary to English, a negative word (not an indefinite) is used in a Spanish sentence that contains **no** meaning *not*. An indefinite word cannot appear in a negative Spanish sentence.

English   *I do **not** have **anything**.*
                        | |
                       not   indefinite word

Spanish   **No** tengo **nada**.
                    | |
                   not   negative word *(nothing)*

The following formula for indefinite and negatives in English and Spanish will help you use them correctly.

ENGLISH   **not** + main verb + indefinite word(s)
SPANISH   **no** + verb + negative word(s)

In order to use the indefinites and negatives correctly in Spanish, it will often be necessary to reword the English sentence so that it is a word-for-word translation of the Spanish sentence.

*I do **not** see **anybody**.*
   | |
  not + indefinite

No veo a **nadie**.
 | |
no + negative
[word-for-word: "*I do **not** see **nobody**"*]

Follow these steps to find the Spanish equivalent of an English sentence with *not* + an indefinite word:

1. Locate the indefinite word in the English sentence.
2. From the chart choose the negative word that is the opposite of the English indefinite word.
3. Restructure the English sentence using *not* + the negative word chosen under #2 above.
4. Put the sentence into Spanish.

Let us apply the steps outlined above to the following sentences.

*I do **not** want to eat **anything**.*
   1. IDENTIFY THE INDEFINITE: anything
   2. SELECT THE NEGATIVE: nothing
   3. RESTRUCTURE: "I do not want to eat *nothing*"
No quiero comer **nada**.

*I don't (do **not**) know **anyone** here.*

1. IDENTIFY THE INDEFINITE: anyone
2. SELECT THE NEGATIVE: no one
3. RESTRUCTURE: "I don't know *no one* here"

No conozco a **nadie** aquí.

▼▼▼▼▼▼▼▼▼▼▼▼▼▼▼▼▼▼▼▼REVIEW▼▼▼▼▼▼▼▼▼▼▼▼▼▼▼▼▼▼▼▼

Underline the indefinite word or phrase in the following sentences.
- Select the negative word that is the opposite of the English indefinite word.
- Restructure the English sentence using **no** + the negative word chosen above.
- Fill in the negative phrase in the Spanish sentence.

1. I'm not going to do that ever.

    NEGATIVE: _____

    RESTRUCTURE: _____

    No voy a hacer eso _____

2. John isn't going to the party either.

    NEGATIVE: _____

    RESTRUCTURE: _____

    Juan no va a la fiesta _____

3. We don't have anything to do.

    NEGATIVE: _____

    RESTRUCTURE: _____

    No tenemos _____ que hacer.

4. They don't know anyone in Bogotá.

    NEGATIVE: _____

    RESTRUCTURE: _____

    No conocen a _____ en Bogotá.

ANSWER KEY

1. What is a Noun? 1. student, classroom, teacher 2. Wilsons, tour, Mexico 3. figure skating, event, Winter Olympics 4. Buenos Aires, capital, Argentina, city 5. truth, fiction 6. manager, intelligence, sense, humor

2. What is Meant by Gender? 1. M 2. ? 3. F 4. ? 5. ? 6. F 7. ?

3. What is Meant by Number? 1. P 2. S 3. S 4. P 5. P 6. S

4. What are Articles? 1. los 2. una 3. unas 4. el 5. un 6. las 7. unos 8. una 9. la

5. What is the Possessive? 1. the parents of some children 2. the office of the doctor 3. the speed of a car 4. the soccer coach of the girls 5. the mother of Gloria Smith

6. What is a Verb? 1. purchase 2. were 3. enjoyed, preferred 4. ate, finished, went 5. was, to see, struggle, to get 6. attended, to celebrate

7. What is an Infinitive? 1. to do 2. study 3. to learn 4. sing 5. to travel

8. What are Auxiliary Verbs? 1. will 2.— (*are* is a Spanish auxiliary and is expressed with **estar**) 3. did 4.— (*had* is a Spanish auxiliary and is expressed with **haber**) 5. do

9. What is a Subject? 1. Q: What rang? A: The bell. (S) Q: Who ran out? A: The children. (P) 2. Q: Who took the order? A: One waiter. (S) Q: Who brought the food? A: Another. (S) 3. Q: Who voted? A: The first-year students (*or* The students). (P) 4. Q: What assumes? A: That. Q: Who is always right? A: I. (S) 5. Q: Who says? A: They. (P) Q: What is a beautiful language? A: Spanish. (S)

10. What is a Pronoun? The antecedent is between parentheses. 1. she (Mary); him (Peter) 2. they (coat, dress) 3. herself (Mary) 4. we (Paul, I) 5. it (bed)

11. What is a Subject Pronoun? 1. yo 2. 0 3. nosotros *or* nosotras 4. 0 5. ellos 6. ellas

12. What is Meant by Familiar and Formal "You"? 1. ustedes / ustedes 2. tú / tú 3. usted / usted 4. vosotros / ustedes 5. tú / tú 6. usted/ usted

13. What is a Verb Conjugation? STEM: compr- CONJUGATION: yo compro; tú compras; él/ella/Ud. compra; nosotros compramos; vosotros compráis; ellos/ellas/Uds. compran

14. What are Affirmative and Negative Sentences? Words that indicate the negative are in *italics*. Words that would not appear in the Spanish negative sentence are found at the end of the sentence. 1. We *do not (don't)* want to leave class early. *do not (don't)* 2. He *did not (didn't)* do his homework yesterday. *did not (didn't)* Teresa *will not (won't)* go to Chile this summer. *will not (won't)* 4. Robert *cannot (can't)* go to the restaurant with us. *cannot (can't)* 5. Mr. Smith *does not (doesn't)* play tennis every day. *does not (doesn't)*

15. What are Declarative and Interrogative Sentences? Words that indicate the interrogative are in *italics*. Words that would not appear in the Spanish interrogative sentence are at the end of the question between parentheses. 1. *Did* Richard and Kathy study all evening? *(did)* 2. *Does* your brother eat a lot? *(does)* 3. *Do* the girl's parents speak Spanish? *(do)*

16. What are Some Equivalents of "To Be"? 1. CHAR ser 2. COND estar 3. COND estar 4. CHAR ser 5. COND estar 6. COND estar 7. CHAR ser

18. What is the Present Tense? 1. reads 2. is reading; **lee** 3. does read; **lee**

19. What is the Past Tense? IMPERFECT: was, was checking, was handling, was crying, was, was leaving PRETERITE: went, arrived, ran, dropped, tried, ducked, grabbed, brought, comforted, smiled, got

20. What is a Participle? 1. P 2. PP 3. I 4. PP 5. P

21. What is a Progressive Tense? 1. P 2. PG 3. PG 4. P 5. P

23. What is the Subjunctive? 1. S 2. S 3. I 4. S 5. S 6. S 7. I

24. What is the Imperative? I. 1. Study every evening. 2. Let's go to the movies once a week. II. 1. Don't sleep in class. 2. Don't talk a lot. III. 1. I 2. I 3. P 4. I 5. I 6. P

25. What are the Perfect Tenses? 1. had gone → PSP 2. has left → PP 3. will have graduated → FP 4. would have studied → CP; had remembered → PSP 5. have seen → PP

26. What is the Future Tense? 1. will study, study 2. '11 clean, clean 3. shall leave, leave 4. won't (will not) finish, finish 5. will be, be

27. What is the Conditional? 1. C 2. C, IS 3. C *or* IS 4. P, F 5. C 6. PS, CP

28. What is a Reflexive Verb? 1. se 2. me 3. nos 4. te

29. What is Meant by Active and Passive Voice? 1. cow, cow → A, PS 2. bill, Bob's parents → P, PS 3. bank, bank → A, P 4. everyone, everyone → A, F 5. spring break, all → P, F

31. What is a Descriptive Adjective? The noun or pronoun described is between parentheses. 1. young (man), Spanish (newspaper) 2. pretty (she), red (dress) 3. interesting (it) 4. old (piano), good (music) 5. tired (Paul), long (walk)

32. What is a Possessive Adjective? The noun possessed is between parentheses. 1. my (book), S → **mi** 2. your (boots), P → **tus** 3. his (mother), S → **su** 4. our (children), P → **nuestros**

33. What is an Interrogative Adjective? The noun modified is between parentheses. I. 1. which (book) 2. what (exercises) 3. which (house) II. 1. how many (shirts) P → **cuánta** 2. how much (wine) S → **cuánto** 3. how many (telephones) P → **cuántos** 4. how much (salad) S → **cuánta**

34. What is a Demonstrative Adjective? The noun modified is between parentheses. 1. that (restaurant), S → **ese** 2. those (houses), P → **aquellas** 3. these (shoes), P → **estos** 4. this (magazine), S → **esta**

35. What is Meant by Comparison of Adjectives? The noun modified is between parentheses. 1. older (teacher) → C+ 2. less intelligent (he) → C- 3. as tall as (Mary) → C= 4. the worst (boy) → S 5. better (student) → C+

36. What is an Adverb? The word modified is between parentheses. 1. early (arrived) 2. really (quickly), quickly (learned) 3. too (tired) 4. reasonably (secure) 5. very (well), well (speaks)

37. What is a Conjunction? The words to be circled are in parentheses. 1. Mary (and) Paul were going to study French (or) Spanish. 2. She did not study (because) she was too tired. 3. Not only had he forgotten his ticket, (but) he had forgotten his passport as well.

38. What is a Preposition? 1. about 2. from, by 3. around 4. contrary to 5. between

39. What are Objects? 1. Q: The children took what? A: A shower. → DO 2. Q: They ate what? A: The meal. → DO Q: They ate in what? A: In the restaurant. → OP 3. Q: He sent what? A: A present. → DO Q: He sent a present to whom? A: His brother. → IO

40. What is an Object Pronoun? The words to be underlined are in parentheses. 1. (it) DO, DO, book → S, **lo** 2. (them) DO, DO, magazines → P, **las** 3. (them) IO, IO → P, **les** 4. (him) IO, IO → S, M, **le**

41. What is an Interrogative Pronoun? The words to be underlined are in parentheses. 1. (whose) P, Of whom is the sweater → **de quién** 2. (who), O, To whom are you talking → **quién** 3. (who), S → **quiénes**

42. What is a Demonstrative Pronoun? The antecedent is between parentheses. 1. this one (house) → S, NS, **ésta** 2. that one (notebook), → S, NPS, **ése** 3. those over there (houses) → P, A, **aquéllas**

43. What is a Possessive Pronoun? The antecedent is between parentheses. 1. mine (car) → S, **el mío** 2. hers (parents) → P, **los suyos** 3. yours (boots) → P, **las tuyas** 4. ours (rackets) → S, **la nuestra**

44. What is a Relative Pronoun? The words to be underlined are between parentheses. 1. (that) letter, DO → **que** 2. (who) woman, S → **que** 3. Paul is the student with whom I traveled. (whom) student, OP → **quien** 4. (what) no antecedent, S → **lo que**

45. What are Indefinites and Negatives? The words to be underlined are between parentheses. 1. (ever) never; I'm *not* going to do that *never* → **nunca** 2. (either) neither; John is*n't* going to the party *neither* → **tampoco** 3. (anything), nothing; we do*n't* have *nothing* to do → **nada** 4. (anyone), no one; they do*n't* know *no one* in Bogotá → **nadie**

INDEX